THE FORMATION AND DEVELOPMENT OF THE VIETNAMESE EVANGELICAL CHURCH OVER THE PAST CENTURY

THAI PHUOC TRUONG

HỘI THÁNH TIN LÀNH VIỆT NAM
100 NĂM
Hình Thành và Phát Triển

THE FORMATION AND DEVELOPMENT OF THE VIETNAMESE EVANGELICAL CHURCH OVER THE PAST CENTURY
by Thai Phuoc Truong

Printed in the United States of America

ISBN: 9781092850674

Foreword

Dear brothers and sisters in Jesus Christ:

While preparing for our hundred-year Gospel in Vietnam celebration, the church's board of directors recommended I collect and edit this history book about the churches in Vietnam.

This long-term, complex project requires great accuracy. Thus, to support the far-ranging reach of this book, I only recorded highlights before 1975 and summarized Church activities after 1975 that have never been systematically recorded. The hundred-year anniversary celebration of the Gospel being spoken in Vietnam was held from June 14–16, 2011, in Đà Nẵng city, after which this book was compiled to record the general formation and development of Vietnamese churches throughout the last century.

Because of the tight deadline under which this book was written, it might contain mistakes. I hope you, as my brothers and sisters in God, help me to contribute more information to this project so we can continually improve this endeavor. For the glory of our God, hopefully, Vietnam's churches will continue to grow, and I aspire for this to happen with all my heart.

Amen!

Rev. Dr. Thái Phước Trường.

Table of Contents

THE FORMATION AND DEVELOPMENT OF THE VIETNAMESE EVANGELICAL CHURCH OVER THE PAST CENTURY

A hundred years ago, Vietnam was considered a new and little-known land, and the Gospel was not preached. A century later, Vietnam has made many changes, especially regarding the formation and development of the Vietnamese Evangelical Church. A century has passed, and with it, difficulties in aspects related to economics, politics, and religion. Evil always wanted to submerge the ship of the Church.

But thank God, He still walks among us, preserving and leading the Church to survive and grow to this day, just as Jesus said, "On this rock, I will build my church, and the gates of Hell shall prevail against it" (Matthew 16:18—NIV).

In any society, memories play an important role. If there was no history to support memories, society would become a ghost. Therefore, on the occasion of the first hundred years since Gospel came to Vietnam, this book was collected and compiled to remind us what God has done, with the aim of honoring God's name, so all the peoples of the Earth might know that the hand of the Lord is powerful and so you might always fear the Lord your God." (Joshua 4:24—NIV)

A. PART I: BEFORE THE EVANGELICAL CHURCH CAME TO VIETNAM. Viet Nam in the Early Twentieth Century

Vietnam is 329 square kilometers, and it is located on the Indochina Peninsula in Southeast Asia, which is bordered by China to the north and Laos and Cambodia to the west. To the east, Vietnam is bordered by the South China Sea , with a coastline of 3,260 kilometers. Outside the continent, Vietnam's territory includes islands and an archipelago. Vietnam has a rich, diverse natural resources.

The population in the early twentieth century was around twenty million. It was twenty-five million in the mid-twentieth century, and it is eighty-seven million at present. Vietnam has fifty-four ethnic groups. The largest, at eighty-seven percent of the population, is Kinh. Other minority groups are Ba-na, Chăm, Cơ-ho, Ê-đê, Gia-rai, Hơ-rê, Khơ-me, H'Mông, Mường, Nùng, Sán Dìu, Tày, Thái, Sê-đăng, and Hoa.

I. Vietnamese Political Context

In the late nineteenth century and early twentieth century, Vietnam became a semi-feudal colony and was divided into three parts by the French: Northern, North Central Coast, and Southern. The Northern (Tonkin) was headed by a French envoy. Each province was ruled by a French envoy and feudal Vietnamese mandarin. The North Central Coast was under the rule of emperors from the House of Nguyễn. However, there was still supervision from a resident superior and French envoys. The Southern region was a concession under direct French governance. Hanoi, Haiphong, and DaNang were concession cities. In short, the throne of the House of Nguyen remained at the Hue Capital on the North Central Coast, but only as a puppet. Meanwhile, French colonialists took over the whole Vietnamese territory. These three parts of Vietnam with Cambodia and Laos became French Indochina, under the general government of Indochina. The presence of Protestant missionaries from the United States, Canada, and Germany caused concern to French colonialists, inevitably preventing evangelization in its early stages.

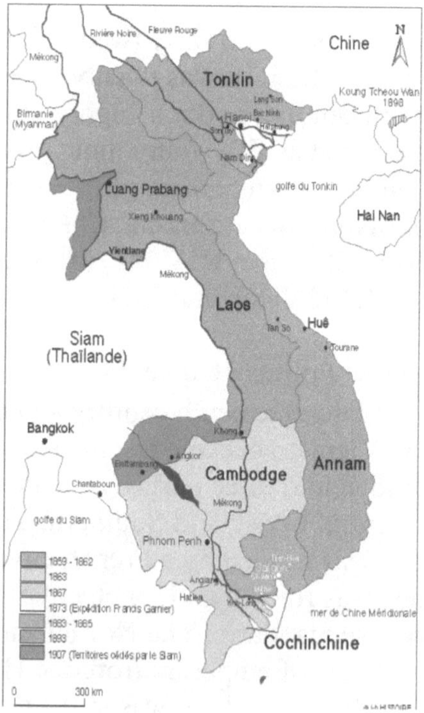

II. Socioeconomic Contexts

In the early twentieth century, Vietnam was still a poor agricultural country, with ninety percent of the population being farmers. The exploitative French colonial policy produced a division of workers for the French plantations and catacombs. For this reason, most people were poor and low-income, except for property owners, merchants, and officials for the French government. Under this French colonial government, cities in Vietnam began to take shape and grow, including Hanoi, Haiphong, SaiGon-Chợ Lớn, NamDinh, Vinh, Hue, Danang, QuiNhon, BienHoa, and MyTho, forming the merchant class of citizens and the lower middle class.

III. Cultural and Educational Contexts

Vietnam's culture was affected by two great civilizations, India and China. In the early twentieth century, French remained the language of feudal education and examination, using mainly Han (Chinese) characters. Nôm (Southern) characters were also popular in this period, some Bibles were translated into Nôm. After the 1910s, because of the area's Confucian background, Chinese characters began to be replaced by Quốc Ngữ characters—the modern Vietnamese characters in use nowadays were produced by Latin characters. The old educational system was replaced in 1915.

After 1917, the French officials opened a new educational system consisting of three levels: beginner, primary school, and high school, at which the following were taught: Hán (Chinese), Quốc Ngữ (which used Latin characters for Vietnamese), and French. From primary school onwards, French was the main language used. However, development of Quốc Ngữ played a very important role that contributed to the Bible's popularity and spread the Gospel.

IV. Religious Context

When coming to Vietnam, missionaries had to face a very complex religious situation, including the presence of Roman Catholics since the sixteenth century. For a thousand years, the area subscribed to common belief with the Vietnamese folk religion and concepts from the triple religions (Vietnamese: *tam giáo*). Triple religions are Mahayana Buddhism, Confucianism, and Taoism.

1. Ancestor Worship (Or Ancestor Veneration)

Ancestor worship is a common Vietnamese religion. According to this traditional belief system, the spirits of people from the afterlife will wander from place to place until they find a resting place provided by their children who are still living. The idea is that life will continue after death. Consequently, sacred duty of descendants (especially the eldest son) is to worship ancestors, report, and plead for the blessing of the deceased. Vietnamese families reserve part of a family's assets, called *đất hương hỏa* (property that belonged to ancestors), so the person who has responsibility for taking care of sacrifices can worship the ancestors. Ancestor worship is often called the "filial piety" of descendants.

2. *Thành Hoàng* Worship (Tutelary Gods)

   Tutelary gods are the gods of every village. They are worshiped in communal houses and temples every month in special events. Each village has its own god. Some villages worship only one god, but others perhaps worship numerous gods. *Thành Hoàng* are predominantly male, and their general nature is to protect the country and to help people.

3. Confucianism

   Confucianism is also known as *Ruism*. It is a political and social doctrine rather than a religion in the true sense of the word. This ideology dominated our country during the feudal period, penetrating all areas of Vietnamese life, from mandarins to civilians. Ruism nowadays still exists in the cultural heritage, customary rituals, and moral counsel. The first clergy members had to face disputes between the Confucian ideology protected by feudal mandarins and the new Western ideology introduced by French colonialists to reinforce colonial expansion.

4. Taoism

Taoism entered Vietnam early in the first millennium AD and was quickly received because there was much attraction to spirits that inhabited rice and worship of the gods. After the ninth century, Taoism turned to such folk arts as witchcraft, magic, and divination. Also worshiped was Thanh Hoang (tutelary gods) and Thanh Mau (the Goddess), as a basis for the formation of religious beliefs of a local nature.

5. Buddhism

Buddhism entered Vietnam very early, around the end of the second century, but really prospered during the Dinh and Tien Le dynasties, especially the Ly and Tran dynasties. Buddhism declined from the post period, especially under the Nguyen dynasty. Gia Long, who was a devout Christian, boldly rejected both Buddhism and Taoism. Buddhism is a religion that has a simple, dynamic creed: Everything depends on predestination. For every method, sentience, condition, and qualification, there are appropriate spiritual practices. At the beginning of the twentieth century, Buddhism fell into a deep recession. The monks could only teach Buddhists how to use the ouija board, draw cards, and go to the fields. People went to the temple just to pray for luck.

6. Roman Catholicism

Roman Catholicism entered Vietnam around the sixteenth century and enjoyed good results until the seventeenth century. However, due to the prohibition and persecution of kings, especially under King Minh Mang, Thieu Tri, and Tu Duc, Roman Catholicism developed very slowly. In fact, until the peace of Giap Tuoc (1874) was signed, Roman Catholics were not seen as a religion and did not have the opportunity to thrive in Vietnam. In their early period, Catholics developed mainly in rural areas in the North and Central regions, then spread to other regions. In the early twentieth century (1910), Catholicism in Vietnam had about 900,000 followers. In the middle of the twentieth century, there were about 1.5 million followers.

Amidst the two world wars, there were two new religions, Cao đài (1926) and Hoa Hao Buddism (1936), which appeared in the south of Vietnam. Approaching such a society with a religious context, as mentioned above, Protestants could not evade the frustrations, distortions, and prohibitions of traditional beliefs and other religions. However, thanks to the grace of God, the devoted sacrifices of priests in the early period, and the following in the creative, wise ways of the servants and children of God, Vietnamese churches grew faster than at any other time.

Roman Catholic in 20th Century

B. Reverend Doctor A. B. Simpson and The Christian and Missionary Alliance (C&MA)

I. Brief profile of Pastor A. B. Simpson:

Pastor A. B. Simpson is the founder of "The Christian and Missionary Alliance" (C&MA) - the Evangelical Union Mission - and plays an important role in bringing the Gospel to Vietnam. He was born on December 15, 1843 in Bayview, on Prince Edward, Canada, in a godly family of the Presbyterian. He actually met the Lord at age 15 and decided to consecrate himself to the Lord. He studied God's words at Knox College, Toronto, graduated in April 1865 and was ordained a pastor two months later. After graduating, in September 1865, Simpson was appointed manager at Knox Presbyterian Church in Canada. He served the Lord here for 8 years. In 1874, he was invited to the Presbyterian Church of Chestnut Street, Louisville, Kentucky, USA. Pastor Dr. A.B. Simpson hired Macauley theater to organize great evangelistic meetings. In November 1879, although his position was very fruitful in Louisville, Pastor Simpson accepted an invitation to serve as the head of the 13th Presbyterian Church in New York, because he wanted to make a missionary vision worldwide, in February 1880, reverend Simpson published a mission magazine called the Gospel in All Lands. This is the first image-based missionary magazine published in North America.

After experiencing the power to heal sickness, the burden of missionary mission to the lost throughout the world had urged Simpson, so in November 1881, he resigned from his position as the Presbyterian Church of the 13th Street. And he started on independent preaching career for New Yorkers. In January 1882, he published the monthly magazine called The Word, The Work and The World mission and a month later he set up the "Evangelistic Tabernacle", cheering on world mission. In October 1882, he officially established a Bible School (1897 moved to Nyack) to train clergies. In November 1884, five of the first 27 students were sent to missionaries in the Congo. Pastor A. B. Simpson did not intend to establish a new denomination, he was only interested in fellowship among those who were passionate about the Lord's Great Commission, joining hands to promote world mission.

So, in 1887, Pastor A. B. Simpson established the Christian Union, the International Missionary Federation. In April 1897, these two associations merged into the Christian and Missionary Alliance (C&MA). He organized many mission conferences throughout the major cities of the United States, attracting hundreds of attendees, calling for a strong dedication to the mission of the Federation of the Evangelical Mission. In 1893, he went to visit missionaries in 12 countries that the Association has sent so he could see the need in those countries that have never heard the Gospel before. The results of the trip were re-presented in his book "Broader Vision of Missionary Areas". By 1895, the Association had attracted hundreds of thousands of people to participate in missionary work and sent nearly 300 missionaries to the most difficult areas yet to hear the Gospel.

In July 1902, he released the first issue of Living Truths magazine, targeting the elite of society. In January 1910, Simpson made a visit to South America, where C&MA missionaries were working. In 1911, he made the last overseas trip of his life in England. In 1912, the annual general meeting in Boone, Lowa, the United States made important adjustments in the Society's charter regarding both doctrinal and organizational issues.

Pastor Simpson fell asleep in the Lord on October 29, 1919, after 76 years of living and faithfully serving His Kingdom.

II. Union of Evangelical Evangelization (C&MA)

The purpose of the Federation of the Evangelical Union is evangelism around the world - the vision of Pastor A. B. Simpson, founder of the Society. Pastor Simpson said, "Please never forget the special call in the work of the Union. We are not called to form a denomination or to repeat a work already done, nor to justify an advocate for a particular theological system, or to honor a good individual. The first task is for everyone to see Jesus, to encourage and urge the children of God to perform the forgotten work of this age for the unbelieving classes in the country as well as peoples who are perishing in foreign countries."

Under the leadership of Pastor AB Simpson and his successors, the Federation of the Evangelical Union promoted, selected, trained and sent clergies to many countries around the world, especially those that had never been listen to the gospel. Today, the number of clerics has surpassed the number of 1,000 and the Association's activities are present in 48 countries.

C. PREPARATION AND ESTABLISHMENT OF THE CHURCH (1887-1911)

I. First Achievements (1887-1911)

In February 1887, Dr. A.B. Simpson, founder of the CM&A, wrote in the magazine *The Word, the Work and the World* as follows: "Free of Southeast Asian peninsula has been neglected. Forget too much noise. Great Kingdom of Annam, together with Tibet should be considered the missionary field of the Association."

Some people believe that Roman missionaries were the first to set foot in Vietnam in the tenth century. In the Le Anh Tong dynasty (1557-1573), a cross was found in an ancient temple. Indeed, although there were once merchants, French Protestant officers worked in Vietnam. E ven the French Protestant church once sent pastors to Hai Phong (1884) to take care of the European Protestants, but the mission for the Vietnamese people was still forgotten.

In 1886, Pastor Boisset called on the French Missionary Association to send clergy to missions in

Vietnam soon because the door was open. However, the French Protestant church ignored the precious opportunity to bring the Gospel to Vietnam. In 1893, Reverend David Lelacheur visited SaiGon and returned to report to Dr. A.B. Simpson in Singapore that the door in Vietnam as well as the entirety of French Indochina was open for preaching the Gospel. Since the French-Vietnamese government at that time only allowed the clergy of French and Spanish Catholics to propagate their religion and other foreign clergy were banned, Dr. A.B. Simpson decided to establish a mission office in Guangxi, South China, to enter Vietnam. Accordingly, God had brought Mr. and Mrs. C.H. Reeves came to Guangxi and waiting for the right time to come into Vietnam.

In 1897, C.H. Reeves crossed the China-Vietnam border to visit Lang Son Province. In 1899, R.A. Jaffray (Figure 3) crossed the China-Vietnam border along the Hồng River to Hanoi but could not set up an office in this place. In 1902, the missionaries thought that people spoke French, which was easier to bring to French Indochina, so they sent Mr. and Mrs. Sylvan Dayan, a French Canadian, to Vietnam. Mr. and Mrs. Dayan went to Hai Phong with plans to open a mission in Tonkin but were arrested by the French government. In the following year, they returned to South China.

Missionary R.A. Jaffray

Missionary Paul M. Hosler

Missionary G. Lloyd Hughes

In 1902, the Bible Society of England established a headquarters in DaNang and published the Bible in Chinese and Nôm, popularly for residents in Quang Nam and Da Nang. In 1905, a mission was set up in Long Chau near Lang Son border in hope of spreading the Gospel. France managed the border very tightly, so the mission was unsuccessful.

On May 25, 1911, Rabbi R.A. Jaffray and two clergymen, Paul M. Hosler (Figure 4) and G. Lloyd

Hughes (Figure 5), traveled to Tourane Port (Da Nang) in Central Vietnam. The French government allowed them to open a mission base in Da Nang city. They bought the headquarters of the Bible Society of England at the corner of Khai Dinh-Nguyen Hoang (now Ong Ich Khiem-Hai Phong) to be the first headquarters of the association.

Choosing Da Nang to be the original headquarters was a wise calculation for the pioneers. In addition to the central geographical position of the whole country, the Central Coast was the least developed for Roman Catholicism. Moreover, Danang was one concession of France, so the formation of a procedure to establish a religion on Bible Society land was an easier way to get the government's permission. Subsequently, the missionaries returned to South China to prepare the way. Thus, 1911 is considered the first year the Protestant Church was transmitted to Vietnam.

II. The First Missionary: Establishing France's Eastern Church (After 1911)

Glad a mission office was established in Da Nang, Dr. A.B. Simpson enthusiastically called on missionaries from North America to Europe to quickly come to the mission field in Indochina. By 1914, there were nine clergy members in Vietnam (one British, two Norwegians, four Canadians, and two Americans). The number of clergies doubled in 1921 and tripled in 1927.

PART II
BETWEEN 1911-1927

From the Date of Establishment to Independence

I. Summary

II. Method to expand evangelism and church activities

1.Preaching with the language of native speakers
2.Dissemination of Gospel literature
3.Developing new facilities
4.Human resource training
5.Council of spirituality and prayer
6.Personal evangelism
7.Facing persecution

PART II

I. Summary

In the summer of 1911, only Hosler returned to Danang. The clergyman Hughes passed away in South China, while Jaffray oversaw China and Indochina. Hosler began to learn Vietnamese and French with Mr. Bonnet and approached local people by distributing the Bible and personal evangelism. At the end of 1912, he reported the baptism of one person. This first believer was Mr. Nguyen Van Phuc, one of the sellers of Gospel literature.

The number of believers gradually increased, and a stable place of worship became necessary. Therefore, on March 30, 1914, after nearly a year of preparation, a branch church was built in Da Nang, the first Evangelical church in Vietnam (Figure 6). On April 5, 1914, the first Sunday school class was opened, with seven learners. In 1914, when there were nine missionaries at the mission headquarters, Hosler opened a mission site in Hoi An (Quang Nam), giving it to Soderberg and Birkel to operate.

The First Church

In early 1915, two new sites were opened in Hanoi and Hai Phong. According to the official report, there were only six members at this time, including one woman, at all locations. The French authorities suspected the German missionaries were spying, so in December 1915, the French governor ordered them to be deported. Only four missionaries remained: Mr. and Mrs. Cad Cadman (Figure 7) and Mr. and Mrs. E.F. Irwin (Figure 8). However, their activities were limited in Da Nang, and all other facilities were closed.

In 1916, R.A. Jaffray went to meet the Governor-General of Indochina in Hanoi to request permission to continue the mission, and the French government gradually eased the ban, allowing clergy to operate at Da Nang, Hanoi, Hai Phong, and Nam Ky. Mr. and Mrs. Cadman's grandparents went to Hanoi to translate and print the Bible.

W.C. Cadman

Mr. & Mrs. I.F.Irwin

The year 1916 marked the beginning of the development of the Danang Church, with twenty-five official members and one Sunday school class. During this time, the members of Hoi An continued to go to Da Nang to worship God and return to Hoi An to testify their faith, bringing many people to God.

Missionary J.D. Olsen

In 1918, the number of members in Da Nang increased to fifty-eight, and they opened another mission site in Hai Chau (South of Da Nang city). In Hanoi, four members were baptized. After World War I, in 1918, the clergy were allowed to return to Vietnam. Some of those, J.D. Olsen and I.R. Stebbins, were sent to Saigon. R.M. Jackson and D.I. Jeffrey were sent to Hai Phong, Mrs. Mary Hartman was sent to Da Nang.

Missionary I.R. Stebbins

At this time, E.E. Irwin was a pastor at the Da Nang Church, and his assistant was Hoang Trong Thua (Figure 13). Mr. Thua was a Confucianist Vietnamese language teacher. He was one of the first followers of the Vietnamese Evangelical Church. He attended the correspondent theological program at Vu Chau Theological College (Wuchow), because no Bible School was taught in Vietnamese in Vietnam. He graduated in September 1924.

Missionary R.M. Jackson

Missionary D.I. Jeffrey

Pastor Hoang Trong Thua

In 1921, the Bible School was opened in Da Nang, led by D.I. Jeffrey, with eight students the first year. John D. Olsen was assigned to translate the Bible and was a great contributor to the compilation of teaching materials at the Bible School.

The Mission Society decided to open three new locations in the South of Vietnam: Sadec (I.R. Stebbins), Chau Doc (R.Z. Grupes), and Can Tho (H.A. Jackson) (Figure 15).

In 1921, the Danang Church had 115 members and became the first autonomous church in Vietnam. In late 1921, with twenty-two clergy and the support of eight Vietnamese Ecclesiastes, the Christian and Missionary Alliance established five bases and eight churches with 183 members.

Missionary H.A. Jackson

The years 1921 to 1927 were a period of rapid development of the Church in Vietnam. The number of missionary establishments increased to ten (1924) and then eleven (1925). The number of missionaries in the province increased to twenty-two (1924), thirty-seven (1925), and sixty-seven (1927). The number of members increased to 1,671 people (1924), 2,939 people (1925), and 4,326 people (1927). In general, the fastest development occurred in Quang Nam, according to the record of Le Van Thai in forty-six years in office. From Hoi An, the Gospel was transmitted along the Thu Bon and Vu Gia rivers to Phong Thu, Lac Thanh, Dai An, Truong An, and Thu Bon, Khanh Binh, Phu Lanh, Thanh Quit, and Tam Ky.

From My Tho, a series of other churches were formed, including Ben Tre, Go Cong, Tan Thach, Quoi Son, Tan An, Can Duoc, and Loc Thuan.

In Can Tho, churches were developed such as Phong Dien, Cai Rang, O Mon, and Ke Sach.

At the end of 1927, there were 74 churches in Tonkin (North of Vietnam), Central, Southern, and Cambodia, with 4,236 members. Therefore, the General Assembly in 1927 decided to establish a Vietnamese Church independent of the Christian and Missionary Alliance called the Eastern French Evangelical Church.

II. Method of Expanding Missionary Activities and Establishing the Church.

1. Preaching in the Language of Native Speakers

   From the beginning, the missionaries familiarized themselves with customs, especially efforts to learn Vietnamese and preach the Gospel in Vietnamese. Although they were not yet proficient, the native language always attracted listeners, who could easily access the Vietnamese culture and customs. Native language proficiency was always a necessary challenge for clergy in the ministry of Gospel preaching, human resource training, and church expansion.

2. Dissemination of Gospel Literature

   The translation and printing of the Bible was a top priority. In 1914, Cadman began his Bible translation, and by the end of 1915, the gospels of John, Matthew, Mark, Luke, and Romans was translated. In 1918, the translation of the Quoc Ngu script of these books was printed in Shanghai, while the Nôm script was printed in Hanoi.

Mr.&Mrs. Cadman with Vietnamese Bible OT&NT

The rest of the New Testament was translated by Olsen, and the entire New Testament (*Quốc ngữ*, or national script) was printed in Shanghai.

In 1919, Mr. and Mrs. Cadman, in cooperation with the writer Phan Khoi, began translating the Old Testament into Quoc Ngu, a project completed in 1925. In 1926, the entire Bible was printed in Quoc Ngu in a Hanoi printing house.

In addition, other publications such as Sunday school lessons, Bible News, and Personal Evangelism were printed and released to support Bible study, spiritual devotionals, and the spread of the Gospel.

3. Development of New Facilities

After the firm establishment of a local church run by a native pastor, the missionary must leave to establish another facility. Jaffray reminded the missionaries: "Remember that gentlemen are not sent to Vietnam to be good lords, and bishops and gentlemen are also not pastors of these church."

One of the first Protestant facilities

The policy of C&MA was to quickly expand the mission area. In 1918, when the number of clergies increased to nine, the association opened two new facilities, SaiGon and Hai Phong. In 1921, three more South Central states were opened, namely Sadec, Chau Doc, and Can Tho. The following year, Vietnamese churches were also planted in Cambodia for Vietnamese people who worked and lived there.

4. Personnel Training

The policy of the Christian and Missionary Alliance was to establish "an indigenous Church capable of self-reliance, self-management, and self-development." Personnel training was a special focus.

In 1918, a Bible class was held in Danang every day, from noon to 13:30, except Sunday. Notably, this class was offered by new believers like Nguyen Huu Khanh. In September 1921, the Bible School was officially opened in Da Nang, led by missionary D.I. Jeffrey and studying under the Nyack Bible School program. The teaching staff was composed of clergy members like E.F. Irwin, H.C. Smith, J.D. Olsen, and Pastor Hoang Trong Thua. The first course had eight students. In 1924, there were forty-seven students, and in 1927, there were eighty-six students. In 1927, the first eight students graduated and were specially ordained pastors.

In March 1943, Pastor Van Huyen (Figure 18) was appointed as the director, and by 1951, he was appointed the school's true director. The short Bible class was also opened to provide personnel to newly opened groups, such as Mrs. Homer Dixon's (Figure 19). A training class was opened in Hanoi in 1931.

Pastor&Mrs. Ong Van Huyen

Miss Homer Dixon

Missionaries and first students at the Bible School

In 1923, a Bible class for women opened for female staff, pastors' wives, and preachers. A doctrine class on baptism was also organized methodically to equip the new doctrine for new believers before their baptism. The program consisted of twelve weeks, with a rigorous examination. Anyone who was absent for one week had to attend the next course.

Sunday School was also held from the start and was seen as a key measure to help new believers master the doctrine of salvation and testify to their salvation and faith. This program actively contributed to the establishment of an autonomous and self-propagating church in Vietnam.

5. Spiritual Devotionals and Prayer Council

The Spiritual Devotional Council was originally held every year for missionaries to meet, pray, study the Bible, and share their experience with ministry. Since 1924, an annual council has been held in Da Nang for Vietnamese pastors and preachers.

6. Personal Evangelism

Personal evangelism by believers and pastors played an important part in spreading the Gospel and establishing a new Church. This evangelism movement was clearly reflected in the memoir of Pastor Le Van Thai and clergyman I.R. Stebbins.

7. Faced with Persecution

The culture and religious context of Vietnam was a major obstacle for Vietnamese clergy and believers. With the policy of supporting Catholics, the French government and the Nguyen Dynasty persecuted clergy, pastors, preachers, and believers trying to spread the Gospel. In December 1915, the French governor ordered the deportation of German clergy because they were suspected of spying.

The clergy was often troubled by local officials and French envoys. In 1927, the Governor-General of Indochina also stated the position of the French government as follows: "Only Roman Catholic missionaries are free to circulate preaching everywhere." Moreover, Protestant pastors were not given privileges like Catholic priests. The Hue emperor also ordered a ban on evangelism in the Central region. Anyone who disobeyed it would be punished. For example, Pastor Phan Dinh Lieu was arrested in Quang Nam in 1925 while preaching the Gospel.

In general, Protestants were only relatively free and common in the South of Vietnam and the three concessions of France, which were Hanoi, Hai Phong, and Da Nang. The remaining territories were under arbitrary control by local officials.

In addition, distortions of the Gospel made it difficult to develop the faith. In the Central region, the Gospel was called *Gia-tô*. In the North, it was called "confusing religion," and in the South, it was the "American religion." Gossip circulated that anyone attending church would receive twenty dollars, be able to go to the US, or be tax-exempt.

Part III

BETWEEN 1927-1942

FROM INDEPENDENCE TO LEGAL STATUS ISSUED BY INDOCHINA AUTHORITY

A. Organization

B. The Development Process

I. In the North

II. In the Central

III. In the South

IV. Bible School

V. Missionary Work
VI. Facing Arrest and Internal Division

Part III

A. Organization

From 1924 to 1926, the Council was only spiritual and devotional, but after 1927, the Administrative Council was appointed to select the first management board of the Evangelical Church of Vietnam. The General Conference of the General Assembly in 1927 comprised fifty pastors, preachers, and members of the seven self-governed churches and sixty-two branches. Meeting in Da Nang from March 5 to 13, the group established the Independence Evangelical Church with the Christian and Missionary Alliance (C&MA), with the name being the Eastern French Evangelical Church. The first Management Board was elected. It included Pastor Hoang Trong Thua (President), Pastor Tran Dinh (Vice President), Pastor Duong Nhu Tiep (Secretary), Mr. Nguyen Thanh Long (Treasurer), and Pastor Le Van Long (Council Member).

National Church Conference for Administration in 1927 at Da Nang

The General Assembly in 1928 approved the first draft of the Charter and two districts: North-Central County (Tonkin and the northern states) and Southern County (South Vietnam and Cambodia). The county conferences met in Da Nang and My Tho, appointing Pastor Tran Xuan Phan to lead North Central County and Pastor Bui Tu Do to lead South County.

In 1928, the management board also presented the charter to Emperor Bao Dai and the Indochinese Governor General to apply for legal status, but it was not until 1942 that the Governor-General of Indochina signed the recognition decision. The General Council in 1931 decided to divide into three counties: North County (from Thanh Hoa to Hanoi, with Pastor Le Van Thai as leader), Central County (from Nghe An to Ninh Thuan, with Pastor Le Van Long as leader), and Southern County (with Pastor Bui Tu Do as leader).

In 1936, the General Council decided on the church's name: The Eastern Vietnamese French Evangelical Church. The presidents of this section were: Pastor Hoang Trong Thua (1927-1928), Pastor Duong Nhu Tiep (1928-1931), Pastor Tran Xuan Phan (1931-1933), and Pastor Le Dinh Tuoi (1933-1942).

National Church Conference in 1937 at Lac Thanh

National Church Conference in 1938 at Vinh Long

Pastor Hoang Trong Thua
(1927-1928)

Pastor Duong Nhu Tiep
(1928-1931)

Pastor Tran Xuan Phan
(1931-1933)

Pastor Le Dinh Tuoi
(1933-1942)

B. The Development Process in Brief

I. In North Region

The church flourished through the ministry of Pastor Le Van Thai. In 1928, only the Thai pastor's family was sent to the North, but by the start of 1933, there were forty pastors and ministers appointed (mostly from Central Vietnam). As of July 1934, there were 570 believers. In 1933, Pastor Thái focused on missionary work to people in the northern mountainous provinces. The result was very positive, many churches were established. By 1940, North County had fifty-eight branches, compared to fifty-six in Central Vietnam and seventy-five in South County. However, due to the war, twenty-two churches closed in 1941. The rate of baptism in believers of Northern counties was quite low compared to other counties. In 1939, South County had 638 believers who baptized out of 1,479 in total of believers. Central County had 389 believers baptized out of 1,934, in total, and North County had only 99 believers baptized out of 1,248 in total.

Ha Noi Evangelical Church

District Conference in North Region at Lang Son in 1937

II. In Central Region

The Church continued to be consolidated and delivered with the guidance of pastors Le Van Long, Doan Van Khanh, and Ong Van Trung. Many churches opened in Quang Nam, Qui Nhon, Tuy Hoa, Nha Trang, and Ninh Thuan. In 1941, many mature churches were in Phong Thu, Dai An, Truong An, Thu Bon, Phu Lanh, Thanh Quit, Khanh Binh, Phuc Binh, Que Son, Cam Long, Tien Phuoc, Que Phuong, Tra My, Tam Thanh, and Tien Qua. Central County supplied many personnel to North County and South County in this period.

Especially in January 1928, the Bible School sent eight preachers to Hue to testify and distribute Gospel literature, despite a ban on evangelization. In 1931, Hue was allowed to open a group room, and the Church appointed Pastor Hoang Trong Thua to take over the job. The Mission Society also sent D.I. Jeffrey to Hue. Pastor L.R. Stebbins was replaced, he expanded the spread of the Gospel to Thua Thien, Phong Dien, Dien Sanh, Quang Tri, Dong Hoi, Bo Trach, and Khe Sanh.

III. In Southern Region

The church was especially developed in the Central South. From the My Tho base, missionary efforts spread widely to Tan An, Go Cong, An Hoa, Ba Tri, Binh Dai, Loc Thuan, Tan Thach, Quoi Son, Soc Suoi, and Can Duoc. In the early 1930s, P.E. Carlson and Vietnamese pastors bought a ship as a vehicle for preaching the Gospel in the Cuu Long Delta. This missionary ship was used for a long time by Pastor Huỳnh Văn Nga (Figure 21), who traveled through Mỹ Tho to Rạch Giá and brought the Gospel to many people.

Evangelistic Boat

In the South Eastern region, the Church only developed in Bien Hoa and a few other places, because Thu Duc, Ben Cat, fortresses, and Chrau areas were very weak. Particularly in Saigon, in 1927, the clergy rented a good location near the police station and bus station. They opened a church immediately in that place. The room below was used for reading and preaching the Gospel, while the room above was used for teaching the Bible. People from all over visited here to listen to the Gospel, receive the Lord, and bring the Gospel to their homeland. By 1934, the first church was built at 155 Tran Hung Dao.

Sai Gon Church

By the end of 1934, there were thirty-eight churches in North County. In Central County, there were thirty-four. In South County, there were forty-seven. In 1940, the number of churches in North County was fifty-eight, Central County, fifty-six, and South County, seventy-five. In 1941, there were twenty-two missionaries in the Christian and Missionary Alliance, 176 pastors and preachers, 104 churches and branches, and 11,751 members.

IV. Bible School

After six years of establishment (since 1921), Danang Bible School became the largest school in all counties of the CM&A. The number of students in 1928 was ninety-three. In 1929, it was eighty-seven. In 1930, it was ninety-four, and in 1931, it was ninety-two. From 1932 to 1937, the number of students decreased due to the impact of the economic recession. (In 1932, it was forty-two, in 1933, forty-seven, and in 1934, twenty.) After 1938, the number of students increased to112. From 1940 to 1943, there was an average of ninety-two students per year, enough to provide pastors to the counties where they did not have pastor. By 1941, in Vietnam, there was one local missionary or pastor to every twelve believers, which is the highest of all the CM&A's spiritual sites in the world.

V. Missionary Work

During this period, the Vietnamese Evangelical Church developed fully, including such parameters as autonomy, self-sufficiency, and self-propagation. Although the expansion of missionary sites still had the help and advice of the clergy, the work of spreading the Gospel was done mainly by Vietnamese pastors, preachers, and believers. The preaching method started from an established church. Apprentice missionaries and booksellers would visit the surrounding areas and villages to preach, testify, sell the Bible, and distribute tracts. In Quang Nam, believers often did pioneer work. The testimony of their changed lives attracted their friends' attention, and they witnessed during their daily lives, selling clothes, fishing, healing, and doing carpentry.

Dr. Tong Thuong Tiet

Initially, the center of church life was often believers' houses, with neighborhood pastors or preachers organizing the meeting. When the number of believers increased and began to be consecrated, a single church was built, and the County sent a graduate preacher (from Bible school) to be a leader.

Hsaol – K'Ho

The spread of the Gospel in the western waters was also unique. A boat was used to go from house to house along the canals to organize missionary events. The result was that the Church grew very fast. In 1938, the General Assembly was in Vinh Long, and Dr. John Sung came to teach, launching an extensive missionary movement. A Missionary Committee was established in each county and church.

Missionary work was also extended to ethnic minority areas. In 1929, a mission branch was opened in Lang Son for the Turks. In 1932, a mission branch was opened in Hoa Binh for the Muong people and neighboring tribes. In 1929, a clergyman, H. Jackson, went to Da Lat to establish a missionary base. In 1931, Hsaol—the K^Ho ethnic people—believed in God (Figure 23) and later became pastors. From 1930 onward, many missionaries, especially Vietnamese pastors and preachers, volunteered to go on missions to ethnic minority areas. Pastor Travis preached to the Cham people in Phan Rang (1931), Pastor Carlson came to the Chrau people in Xuan Loc (1934). Preacher Ngo Van Lai came to the Bru people in Khe Sanh (1935), and Preacher Nguyen Thuan visited the Paco people in Quang Tri (1940). Preacher Le Khac Cung worked with the M'Nong people in Dak Lak (1940), Preacher Kieu Toan pastored the Ka-tu ethnic people in Quang Nam (1940). Preacher Pham Xuan Tin witnessed to the Gia-rai and Ba-na people in Pleiku.

III. Facing Arrests and Internal Divisions

French governors and Southern dynasties caused difficulties in the Middle and Northern states: A decree on December 26, 1928, of the Privy Council banned evangelism and the Cao Dai religion. In addition, Pastor Le Van Thai was persecuted in the North. Pastor Ong Van Huyen and Preacher Dang Ngoc Cau were arrested on Ly 5 island in May 1928 and detained in Quang Ngai prison.

Around 1930, Pastor Phan Dinh Lieu was arrested again in Nha Trang (Figure 24) and imprisoned for six months in six provincial prisons. He used this opportunity to preach the Gospel to the inmates and translate Christian books from Chinese into Vietnamese.

Subsequently, twenty believers on Que Son island were arrested, and the church's construction was suspended. However, God protected the Church miraculously. The Vietnamese king signed an order to remove the ban on evangelism in Vietnam on January 4, 1929. The French envoy secretly allowed the Church to be active (in Hoi An). People who persecuted the work of God were removed from office or died.

From 1933 to 1936, two pastors who were excommunicated led members to join the Sa Bat Association. After that, large numbers of believers were converted.

Pastor Phan Dinh Lieu (upper right) and prison

PART IV

BETWEEN 1942-1954

FROM LEGAL STATUS TO DESPERATION

A. Vietnam's Historical Background: From 1942 to 1954

B. Church Situation

I. Organization

II. Activities

Part IV

A. Vietnamese Historical Background from 1942 to 1954

The Second World War broke out, and from June 1940 onward, Japan controlled Indochina. In 1945, Japan surrendered to the Allies. British and Chinese troops entered to disarm Japanese troops, and the domestic political situation was very confusing. Accordingly, the Revolution succeeded in August 1945. The State of the Democratic Republic of Vietnam (DRV) was born on September 2, 1945.

The land experienced tragedy in the next few years when a famine in 1945 killed two million people. A war against France lasted nine years, and the Geneva Agreement was reached in 1954, dividing the country into two parts.

B. Church's Situation

I. Organization

In 1941, after Japan came to control Indochina, the Mission Assembly allowed missionaries who did not want to stay to evacuate. Most clergy stayed but were tightly controlled so they could not work. On January 19, 1942, French Governor Jean Decoux signed a decision to recognize the Church's leadership, including pastors Le Dinh Tuoi, Kieu Cong Thao, Bui Tu Do, Le Van Que, Le Van Thai, and Le Van Long.

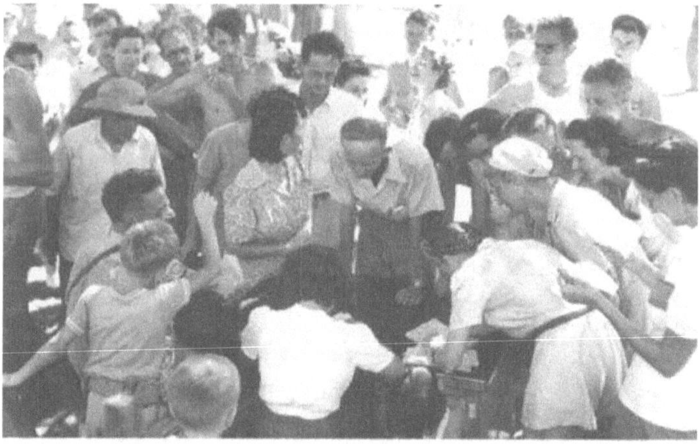

Place missionaries were detained (above photo)
This is where missionaries came out to receive letters from families

This important era marked the growth of the Eastern French Evangelical Church in autonomy, self-governance, and self-sufficiency. Every activity of running the Church and evangelization was carried out by Vietnamese leaders and believers. At this time, the Vietnamese Church did not receive funding from the Mission Assembly, but also supported the clerics who were under house arrest until the end of the Second World War.

In August 1942, the 19th General Assembly in Da Nang (Figure 26) elected Pastor Le Van Thai to be the President. The Council also decided to establish an Evangelical Youth Union organization, strengthen the Preaching Assembly, and launch an extensive missionary program, especially caring for the Montagnard.

National Church Conference at Da Nang

Pastors and Trainees at Bac Viet in 1952

From 1942 to 1945, war and famine struck the land, but no believers died of starvation. Through many challenging situations, the Church became stronger, and the number of believers increased. Eighteen churches were built (nine in South County, four in Central County, and five in Northern County. Twenty-seven branches were self-managed, with all churches self-sufficient by 1945. From 1945 to 1947, because of famine and war, the Church faced great challenges, suffering from both French and Viet Minh (Vietnam Communist) distrust. Many clerics, pastors, and believers were imprisoned or died from war and sickness. War devastated the church, and m any of its locations had to close. About thirty-eight churches closed in South County, with seventeen closed in Central County.

From 1948 to 1954, with the help of the Missionary Assembly, the Church gradually recovered and developed. Pastors and preachers returned to the Church and took care of its sheep amidst the difficult circumstances in the nation. Many believers were added to the three counties, and many missionary facilities and churches were restored. Indeed, the number of believers in 1947 increased from 9,739 to 13,824 in 1954.

In 1950, the General Conference of the CM&A reactivated in Da Nang from 5-9 March. The Council decided the Church's official name was "The Evangelical Church of Vietnam," instead of the old name, "Vietnamese Evangelical Church." Thus, the Church's name changed over many stages:

- 1927: the Eastern French Evangelical Church
- 1936: the Eastern French Vietnam Church
- 1945: the Vietnamese Evangelical Church
- 1950: the Evangelical Church of Vietnam

II. Activities

1. Missionary work

In 1942, the Domestic and Foreign Missionary Assembly arrived. I n 1949, its name was changed to "Vietnam Missionary Assembly" due to Pastor Pham Xuan Tin, the Head Pastor, and Pham Van Nam, the Deputy Head. M any preachers graduated from the Bible School in the Tây Nguyên Highlands. In 1951, Highlands County was established and led by Pastor Hasol. Up to 1954, there were about 3,000 believers, seventy-one churches, ninety-one small branches, and 117 pastors and preachers , supported by thirty-one missionaries from the Missionary Assembly and twenty-one missionaries from Vietnam.

In 1951, the Evangelical Church of Vietnam began evangelizing through the electric wave (Figure 26), that is, the radio in Vien Dong and Manila, Philippines. The Church also continued publishing magazines such as *Lua Thieng* (*Holy Flame*) and *Hung Dong* (*Twilight*), alongside personal preaching and lessons in Sunday School. *The Bible News* was still reprinted in 1950.

Broadcasting Facility

2. Bible School

Although it was difficult, Da Nang Bible School continued its training work. The school was only temporarily closed from 1945 to 1947 due to the fierce war situation. In September 1948, the school reopened with thirty-five students. In 1949, there were 51 students, and in 1950, there were 54 students who met leadership needs, which very much were lacking during the recession (1945-1947).

In 1947, the Bible school in Buon Me Thuot (Figure 28) was built by clergyman G.H. Smith. In 1949, the Bible school in Dalat was built by clergyman H.A. Jackson .

3. Heresy and Internal Division

In 1944, at the Can Tho church, there was a disagreement between believers and Pastor Le Van Ngo, leading to the County disciplining Pastor Le Van Ngo. Ironically, Pastor Le Van Ngo brought many believers to the Seventh-day Adventist Church, leading to conflict afflicting the church. Finally, the government closed the church until 1948, when it reopened.

From 1944 to 1945, Mr. Tran Nhu Tuan, leader of the Vinh church, popularized the incorrect doctrine of the Second Coming. He convinced a large number of believers in Vinh, Ha Tinh, and Hue to follow him. He announced that God would come again on September 30, 1944. When that day came and went, he announced God would return on October 1, 1945.

Many believers sold all their assets and went to the church to wait for God's coming. This caused great damage to the Church, and many believers came to reject the faith.

4. Community Service

In 1953, an orphanage was established in Hòn Chông, Nha Trang (Figure 29) under the leadership of Pastor Le Van Thai.

Protestant Orphanage in Nha Trang

Part V
Between 1954-1975

FROM DESPERATION TO REUNIFICATION

A. The Evangelical Church of Vietnam (North)
B. The Evangelical Church of Vietnam (South)
    I. Organization
    II. Missionary Work
    III. Da Nang Bible School and Nha Trang Theology College
    IV. The Organs of the Church
    V. Publications
    VI. Social and Relief Agencies

Part V

Period 1954-1975

In this period, the country was temporarily divided into two parts, so the Evangelical Church of Vietnam also divided into two separate organizations: the Evangelical Church of Vietnam (South) and the Evangelical Church of Vietnam (North).

A. The Evangelical Church of Vietnam (North)

In 1955, there were only a thousand believers in the North (half migrated to the South), 20 churches, and 13 pastor and preacher families. The Local Council County of 1955 picked Pastor Duong Tu Ap as the head leader, Pastor Hoang Kim Phuc as vice leader, and Mr. Hoang Dinh Giap as secretary. Mr. Au Dang Trinh served as treasurer. In addition, the general assembly of the churches in the north established the Evangelical Church of Vietnam (North), which composed its own charter. In 1963, the Vietnamese Democratic Republic government approved its charter. The leader was Pastor Duong Tu Ap, vice-leader, Pastor Hoang Kim Phuc, and secretary general, Pastor Hoang Dinh Giap.

Pastor Duong Tu Ap

In 1963, the Vietnamese Protestant Church (MB) opened a Bible School in Hanoi, recruiting the first class with 10 students, or three to four per month each year. However, after many years that bible school had been shutting down, the communist agreed to re-open this Bible training school for the northern students in 1988, and there were fifteen students were allowed to enter the new program.

Bible School in Ha Noi between 1988-1993

In 1966, the northern church was governed by the head leader Pastor Hoang Kim Phuc, and his vice leader and secretary general was Pastor Bui Hoanh Thu. At this time, the Evangelical Church of Vietnam (North) had grown slowly compared to the churches in the South. Until 2000s, the North had 6,370 believers, four pastors, ten preachers, and fourteen churches in the province and city.

B. The Evangelical Church of Vietnam (South)

I. Organization

In 1955, the 23rd meeting of General Assembly at Gia Dinh established a Constitutional Amendment Committee. In 1957, the Management Board of the CM&A sent a letter to the government of the Democratic Republic of Vietnam for recognition of its legal status and approval on August 30, 1957.

In 1959, The 27th meeting of the General Assembly at Vinh Long province recognized the Highlands County as part of the Evangelical Church of Vietnam (South).

National Church Conference in 1959

In 1962, The 30th meeting of the General Assembly at Nha Trang decided to divide Central Region into two parts: North Central Region and South Central Region, for four total counties.

Board of General Assembly in 1971

In 1969, the 36th meeting of the General Assembly of the CM&A at Nha Trang decided to divide South Region into two parts: from South East to South West (Mỹ Tho province—Cà Mau province). At the same time, Highland Region was also divided into Central Highland Region (Quảng Trị province and Quảng Đức province) and South Highland Region (Đà Lạt, Bình Long, Phước Long, and Xuân Lộc).

In 1973, The 39th meeting of the General Assembly of the CM&A decided to separate the South West into two: Tiền Giang province (South Central County) and Hậu Giang (South West County). There were then seven counties.

In 1975, the Evangelical Church of Vietnam had 530 churches,146,089 believers, 190 pastors, 167 preachers, and 155 preachers in training.

The head leader of the CM&A from 1942-1975 consisted of Pastor Lê Văn Thái (1942-1960) and Pastor Đoàn Văn Miêng (1960-1975).

Pastor Le Van Thai
(1942-1960)

Pastor Doan Van Mieng
(1960-1975)

2. Missionary Work

During this period, the Church focused on missionary work. Evangelization was conducted in many ways, such as personal preaching, preaching in workplaces, the military, hospitals, youth, students, and children. The Church used as many ways as possible, carrying out campaigns in the city and with missionary boats.

In 1955, a mission was carried out on the Saigon Radio Station. By the year 1965, there were fifteen radio stations, including an evangelical radio show that was thirty minutes long. In total, there were 51 programs a week.

In 1969, there was an evangelistic event on the radio. Evangelical cars were established from 1956 to

1957, and in 960, the Commission for Evangelization for Children was established. In 1966, the CM&A organized a great preaching campaign from June 2 to June 10 at Cộng hòa Stadium in Saigon.

Evangelistic Van

Evangelization for minorities in the Central Highlands also was a focus. Many pastors and preachers from the Kinh people preached to ethnic minorities. In 1959, when Highland County was recognized as the county of the Evangelical Church of Vietnam, there were 133 churches and over 30,000 believers.

Evangelistic Campaign at Cong Hoa Stadium in 1966

In 1962, the Vietnamese General Confederation of Evangelical Churches (VGCEC) established the Central Missionary Committee to run all the work to preach to ethnic groups. In 1973, the VGCEC established the Missionary Group for ethnic minorities of the South Highland, with Pastor Ha Sao A. the leader. Consequently, in 1975, among the ethnic people in the West Highlands, there were 60,000 believers, 216 churches, 42 pastors, 91 preachers, and 50 preachers in training.

3. Da Nang Bible School and the Nha Trang Theological Institute

Da Nang Bible School continued its personnel training. In the academic year 1955-1956, there were 60 students. The number of students in the following years were 82 (1956-1957), 89 (1957-1958), and hundred (1958-1959). During this period, the Preaching Teachers Groups was mostly composed of

Vietnamese. The school was run entirely by Vietnamese people, and missionaries just attended for training.

In 1960, the Bible School was moved to Nha Trang and changed its name to the Theological Bible Institute. In 1960-1961, the institute had 85 students and 55 preachers on probation. In 1975, the institute had 200 male and female students. Pastor Van Huyen was the principal, Pastor Le Hoang Phu, the School Registrar. The curriculum was upgraded, and there was a huge library serving professors and students.

Students Graduated at Da Lat Bible School in 1972

Bible schools in Buon Me Thuot and Da Lat also continued training clergy to serve the Lord and preach to minorities' churches.

An Education Christian Committee was established to research and advise the General Confederation on the education program at the theological institutes, Bible schools, and primary Bible school.

4. Agencies of the Church
   In this period, the Church organized many agencies, such as:

- Committee of the Evangelical Social Relief (1956)
- Committee to Promote Scholarship (1956)
- Christian Youth Union (1957)
- Nursing Committee (1957)
- Commission of Preaching (1957)
- Sunday School Committee (1957)
- Christian Chaplain Committee (1958)
- Christian Student Group (1959)
- Commission for Evangelization for Children (1960)
- Radio Commission (1961)
- Extensive Missionary Committee (1963)
- Education Christian Committee (1968)

5. Publications

Gospel printing houses were moved to Saigon and enthusiastically published works like the full and partial Bible, hymnbooks, preaching books, textbooks, and journals such as *Thanh Kinh Nguyet Sang, Rang Dong, Niem Tin,* and *Duoc Thieng*. By 1966, the printing house had printed 42.2 million pages.

Christian Materials

6. Social and Relief Agencies

In this period, the Vietnamese Evangelical Church was interested in social work. A social relief committee was founded in 1956.

- A Christian clinic was established and operated in 1961 in Hon Chong.
- The leprosy hospital in Buon Me Thuot was established in the year 1951.
- Pleiku Hospital was established in 1969.
- Dalat Hospital was founded in 1959.
- Bethlehem Primary School was founded in 1957.
- Da Nang Primary School was established in 1961.

Evangelistic Clinic

The leprosy hospital in Buon Me Thuot was established in the year 1951.

Pleiku Hospital was established in 1969. Dalat Hospital was established in 1959.

Bethlehem Primary School was founded in the year 1957.

Da Nang Primary School was established in 1961.

Leprosy Hospital

Bet-le-hem School

Part VI
Between 1975-2001

FROM REUNIFICATION TO LEGAL STATUS

A. The Crisis

B. Strengthening

Part VI

For 64 years of its formation and development, the Evangelical Church of Vietnam underwent many ups and downs and entered a very special stage of the country's history and the history of the Church: the event of 1975. This crisis meant many of the Lord's servants and believers had to change their lives. Some had to leave their families and churches to enter the new economy or return to the homeland to live. Several others left the country to settle abroad, changing the life of the church in the cities and country sides. Many believers were down and weak. Less fearful people had left God. A few pastors and preachers also left their positions in this time period. Church activities were limited. The government allowed many churches only to operate in the mornings or on Sunday. Over 200 churches and facilities of the common church like the Theology Institute, Bible School, orphanage, hospital, school study, bookstore, and printer were closed, leveled, or requisitioned. Evangelists were not allowed to testify to their religion. Nor was personal preaching or preaching campaigns allowed.

It was difficult for the Church to exist and develop because of the restrictions on human thought. A foreigner might well think: "In such a country, how can the Church even exist?" By the grace and power of God, the church has not only existed but also thrived. Thank God!

A. The Crisis

During this period, the church was in crisis in many aspects: mental and physical, organizational, facilities, the spiritual life of the church, etc. In this era, there were too many changes and novelties. We will take an honest look to see what was lost and what was achieved.

First, we will mention the losses after the 1975 event. Just before April 30, 1975, the situation in Vietnam was very unstable, so many people were insecure and confused, not only because of the lasting war and complicated political situation but also due to fear for the country's future. Accordingly, many people attempted to leave the country. The church was greatly affected. Clerics were about to leave Vietnam. Many of God's servants and believers also left for many reasons. Some had to stay. Some hesitantly remained in Vietnam, though many were determined to stay in Vietnam, dead or alive, for the Church. Besides, the war situation became even fiercer, complicating many plans of the Church, including its preaching campaigns, all of which stalled.

The transition period before and after the 1975 event caused many of God's children to focus on dealing with the situation rather than having a plan for the church. Even church leaders pondered whether they should go or stay in the country. Some churches were destroyed by the war, and some churches could not function because most of their believers had to evacuate to the city. The Church faced many difficulties, it took a long time to ask the government to re-establish their activity. The time finally came. The Civil War (North and South War) ended on April 30, 1975. Vietnam entered a new era, which was also a special stage of the Evangelical Church of

Vietnam, with so many happy, challenging, bitter events, sorrows, and reasons to be grateful.

Event in April 30th, 1975

I. Personnel

When the 1975 event happened, many servants and children of God left Church activities for many different reasons. Churches lacked personnel, and people were concerned with whether to stick around or leave the Church, due to the following reasons:

a. Homecoming. During the war, many families and individuals left their homeland to live in urban or other places. After 1975, they returned to the fatherland to rebuild their careers. They had to leave the Church, whereas they were attached to their long service to God, leading to many losses and regret for the Church.
b. New economy: The State's policy was to bring many families from the cities to places because of the "new economy" to produce labor. These were not just poor people, but rich families with status in the previous society. Among those were many Christians (Protestants), who had to leave the churches where they had contributed effort and money for a very long time.
c. Changed educational system: Before 1975, many Protestants (followers of the CM&A) were officers, soldiers in the army, and officials of the government—that is, all targets of reform—targets that included pastors and preachers. During their long time away from family and church, some people died in reform camps, and some returned. The latter returned to the country in addition to the guaranteed areas. During this time, their economic situation was also very difficult. The Church lost many personnel.

d. Crossing the border: After 1975, because of the economic and political situation, many people tried to cross Vietnam's border to immigrate to other countries. Some left with their families or traveled alone with the hope their new homes would guarantee their family's passage. Those who remained in Vietnam were just waiting for the opportunity to leave, so there was no direction to their lives. All this greatly influenced the church. Even some pastors and ministers left their positions in the church to escape. Due to pressure, the Board of Management was forced to remove the servants of God that left their position to go abroad. Although in principle, that was not wrong, such decisions were emotionally draining. Most believers understood and sympathized. Still others did not understand. They felt sad and angry. Their grievances surfaced in their relationship with their homeland church later. Many believers who were trained to be very effective personnel in the church also left. Subsequently, Vietnamese people allowed to guarantee their family did so, and the latter left to reunite with them, disappointing the Church's personnel a great deal.

e. Weak people, leaving God: After the 1975 accident, one of the issues that made Protestants in particular and religious followers in general fear was that they did not know if the new regime would have religious freedom of belief. In fact, many officials then were very prejudiced and new little about religion, which caused many misunderstandings among believers. Regrettably, many people did not stand up to this test of faith, so they left God or were very afraid when they claimed to be a Protestant believer at work. Others found life too difficult materially, and their spirits fell accordingly. Their spiritual health was weak, and when they returned to the Church, they created problems in it.

Some believers were arrested: In general, after the accident of 1975, the political situation changed, affecting society and the Church of the day. Soon after 1975, the new contexts had many doubts, and many people were suspected of religious activities. Of course, some people benefited from their religious affiliations, but mostly, people lived the faith in which they truly believed. In this period, some servants and children of God were arrested for religious matters such as being accused of illegal religious activity and violating the law. Sometimes, the bias was just prejudice or a misunderstanding, because there was no clear legal framework for religion.

g. Those who do not want to serve: Some believers stood firm with the Church but did not want to participate in important offices, because they feared trouble from the government or problems with their business or career. Such fears only exacerbated the crisis.

II. Facilities

After 1975, over 200 churches and church facilities were no longer active for various reasons: the church was closed, leveled, or used for government purposes. The government had many misunderstandings regarding churches and their facilities. For example, in one church, there was a room containing weapons (fortunately, it was a lake for baptism). If a pastor violated a government or border crossing, that church and facility would be requisitioned by the State. In some places in rural or remote areas, because of the new situation, government policy was not clear. Due to prejudice from local officials, some churches and facilities were not allowed to operate. Most Bible schools on the campuses of churches were requisitioned by the government, so the activities of those churches were greatly affected. Accordingly, the Church lost their facilities and land attached to the facilities above, including classrooms that were used for Sunday schools. Notably, all the churches and their base were built in in the 1950s and 1960s. After 1975, all this slowly degraded while the number of believers increased, so there was not enough room for worshiping God and living. Meanwhile, the new repairs and construction were not easy because of the lack of finances and permission. In addition, the church needed many other facilities to maintain its operations and develop, such as a theological institute, Bible school, orphanage, printing house, Christian clinic, or school. Most were requisitioned or not activated. For this reason, the basic problems of the Church after 1975 have been discussed with the government to this very day.

Church being changed into Cultural Hall

Former Bible School being changed into College

Another issue for pastors and believers was that some pastors had temporarily resided in church establishments but refused to return them. They wanted to stay there forever to turn into their own property, while many children of God made great sacrifices to give to the Church. The actions of those who do not fear God was a stain on the history of the Evangelical Church of Vietnam that we should not imitate.

III. Organization

According to the organization of the former Vietnamese Evangelical Church, the General Council of the General Confederation and County has been held every year. Therefore, after 1975, although the situation of the country completely changed, the Church still maintained its activities. From June 13 to 15, 1976, the 42nd General Council was held in Saigon Church, even with the new situation of the country, with its advantages and disadvantages.

Elected Composition of the Board of the General Assembly

Head leader	Pastor Ong Van Huyen
Vice leader	Pastor Doan Van Mieng
Secretary	Pastor Nguyen Son Ha
Treasurer	Pastor Le Van Phai

Council Members

Middle Central	Pastor Nguyen Xuan Vong
South Central	Pastor Le Dinh To
South East	Pastor Nguyen Thanh Hang
South Central	Pastor Tang Van Hi
South East	Pastor Nguyen Huu The

Leader of the Youth Committee Pastor Le Khac Hoa

Chairmen

Middle Central County	Pastor Ma Phuoc Minh
South Central County	Pastor Pham Xuan Tin
South East	Pastor Pham Van Thau
South Central	Pastor Nguyen Van Xuyen
South West	Pastor Nguyen Lam Ma

In the history of the Vietnamese Evangelical Church, Pastor Van Huyen had to be head leader for nearly one-fourth century because they could not organize any meeting of the General Assembly nor gain government recognition, because there was no legal entity recognized by the government. Therefore, this was a difficult period for the leadership of the Board of General Management. Most of the members of the General Federation and the County Leaders passed away or retired, and a few of the remaining members had to continue being in charge. Pastor Ong Van Huyen was weak and blind, but he had to lead the Church through an extremely challenging and arduous time for a long while.

After 1975, conducting the work of the Evangelical Church in Vietnam was no longer as easy as before because of many geographic limitations, including moving from one province to another to perform religious activities, pastoral activities, or the many other events required to apply for permission.

In 1976, the District Council, or the General Council of the Federation, no longer existed because the government did not recognize the legal status of the Vietnamese Evangelical Church. Pastors, preachers, and believers did not meet as regularly for fellowship as they had before. The relationship between the General Federation, the County, and the Church was not as easy and convenient as before. Whenever there was a need to contact the government to present needs, or solve problems related to the Church in the localities, the General Federation or County at that time had many administrative difficulties. This was because of the uneven policies and the absence of freedom of government for the churches with no legal status.

Conversely, the churches did not contact the General Federation or their County regularly to solve the difficulties in their localities, not to mention that, in some cases, the localities decided not to comply with rules. Many churches did not comply with the organization or the provisions of their charter. The churches applied rules loosely. Believers, deacons, pastors, and preachers did not know the rules or apply them thoroughly. Sometimes, they did not want to lose the affection of their constituencies or were making up for the situation of that time. Most churches made little mention of the disciplinary issue, which most importantly severed the relationship of believers with their churches, affecting both the organization and the spirituality of the churches. Because of the lack of servants of God, the clergy was not penalized as it should have been, causing stumbling blocks among believers, a lack of fear for God, and respect for the organization's hierarchy. Later, when the order of discipline in the Church was reestablished, the General Federation and the Church met many difficulties from those who were not disciplined because of their disobedience. Thus, it was necessary to consolidate the Church's organization.

Moreover, in this period, most of the churches were less likely to hold an Annual Council to re-appoint deacons and remain in office because of the difficulties within the Church and toward the politicians whenever they organized the Council. Although many deacons committed violations, the Church did not remove them from office.

Many of the churches' operating licenses were confiscated by the government, so the administration also faced difficulties whenever they needed a license. Even some churches that were licensed could not be used because the authorities did not recognize the licenses as legitimate.

At that time, transportation was difficult. Information from the General Federation to the County, and to the churches flowed very slowly. The economy was very limited, so it was impossible to organize any events. There was so much to do yet, so little got done. Sometimes, the church was not strong enough to decide between obeying God and obeying people. So, even if they knew following the organization was wrong, it was sometimes acceptable. Therefore, the organization of the Church at that time experienced many crises.

Moral life in society declined as people focused more on materialism, which greatly affected the Church. In the early Church, as new people joined, the earthly world was also brought into the church. However, since 1975, the way believers and leaders treated each other worsened. Because followers lacked a fear of God, their obedience was reduced. The circumstances created a spirit of "Everyone should live how they want." Sometimes, because of the fear of being related to others, people refused to help each other. Besides, the devil had scattered suspicion to lead to division within the people of God.

IV. Bible, Christian Literature

Since 1975, because of the Christian printing house, the Christian bookroom was not operated. Therefore, spiritual books, studies, hymns, and other written works were not printed. Publishing the Bible was also not allowed, so the lack of scriptures and hymns in worship activities was very serious. The Bible became extremely precious because, even if money could buy it or it was kept well, it would be lost. Indeed, in many places, governments confiscated the Bible because it was illegal. Because the need was indispensable at that time, the children of God in many different ways secretly found a way to get the Bible, hymns, and essential documents for worshiping God. Other ways of worship included studying the Bible. Some people even had to accept handwriting to help them understand the word of God.

The specials (monthly magazines), such as the *Bible News*, *The Dawn*, *Belief*, *Water Live*, *Lecture* and *Life*, were important for many members of the Church, including those who believed that the Church had previously not existed.

Sunday School (one of the most effective and regular faith-building programs of the Vietnamese Evangelical Church) faced many obstacles because it could not be printed. Previously, small books called "Personal Preaching" supported preaching and evangelism. They were now completely unprinted and unpublished.

Documents, records, and information from the General Confederation, which needed to be disseminated to the Assembly, were also very limited. Therefore, this was a great challenge for the servants of God, and it required them to rely on God more in the study of teaching. This was because books and documents were not the same as they had been before.

The lack of such materials and books made the servants of God more serious in building up their faith. There were some books from abroad, translated from foreign languages, but not standardized doctrines. Evil tracts were being widely disseminated in the church. This caused many consequences for the faith of God's children.

V. Training

In the very first stage of the Church, the training of the Lord's servant was a primary goal of the clergy. In 1919, the first Bible class was held in a stables, and in 1921, the Bible School in Da Nang was established. Since 1960, the facility in Nha Trang was renamed the Theological Seminary. After that, the Bible School in Dalat and Buon Me Thuot for ethnic people was established. From these Bible schools, many pastors and ministers were trained to meet the needs of the Church for a long time. In addition, the County annually organized Primary Bible School courses for believers to learn the Word of God more deeply and systematically. Moreover, the Church had training programs depending on its own needs. After 1975, the above training programs were not possible because the Theological Seminary was shut down by the communist government, both the closure of Bible Schools, and banned of Primary School courses.

Most churches were only active on Sundays, trying to keep the Sunday School classes, the Bible's original Bible studies, and mostly the teachings of the Lord's servants in worship services. Training programs that were long-term, large-scale, and intensive were difficult to implement in the early years after 1975. If so, it was only occasionally or quietly organized. However, when the above opportunities were gone, the children of God started to desire for God's words to increase more than before. This was both a need and a challenge for the general Church to have a direction for the training of God's servants in the new period.

Buon Me Thuot Bible School

As mentioned in the previous section, because the staff in the church felt disappointed , initiates were not familiar with the need to be trained and gradually got used to problems. They only served for a while, and then they left. Accordingly, training was a very important task, but believers also faced many difficulties.

Because the Theological Seminary and the Bible schools were no longer active, the preachers and trainee preachers did not have the opportunity to return to school to continue the graduation course, so they were limited in serving God, especially not-yet ordained pastors according to regulations. They could not fully serve the ministry like a true pastor. During this period, the pastor and preachers lacked seriousness, so it was normal for the pastors to serve many churches. This, of course, limited the development of the church. For those who wanted to learn God's words for the service, they had to sacrifice more and pay more because their lives were so difficult. Those were the conditions for the people in the country, and the need for overseas students to receive training was a bigger problem.

VI. Missionary Problem

One of the factors contributing to the survival and development of the Church was the missionary. This is also the great commandment of the Lord: The Church must enable the Gospel of God to be preached to all levels of society. However, after 1975, the missionary campaigns, the weekly evangelical work of the churches, the single preacher's work, the preaching Gospel program on radio stations, prisons, hospitals, schools, universities, hotels—all were banned. In history, the Church had faced many difficulties from before the Gospel's events to Vietnam so far. This, though, was the most widespread difficult period because Gospel preaching was considered a violation of the law, or pastors were told preaching was illegal.

The Church of God was facing great challenges in carrying out His commands. Certainly, God had a good plan for the Church and put in believers' heart the Lord's revelations for this mission. In the view of humans, the churches were in a pessimistic situation. In the past, there were many opportunities and means. The Church had not yet achieved its expectations or objectives in evangelization. Looking back at the history of reformation, the mission to Vietnam had been stalled for a long time because it needed to consolidate its internal problems before its many attacks. After that, many mission teams were established, and the clergy members were sent, albeit with many difficulties.

After 1975, many people had an incorrect and unfriendly view of religion, particularly for Protestants. Many native people believed Protestantism was an American religion or just maybe had a relationship with the USA, so they were reserved. The differences between theism and atheism were not understood in the right way regarding the government's policy about freedom of religion and belief. There were many deviant views of religion in general and Protestant in particular, so evangelization met many difficulties. On their identity card's profile, many people were also afraid to be responsible for declaring that they "have a religion" because it was detrimental to their business, study, or development opportunities. Therefore, the spirit of evangelism within God's children also had negative effects. Some people said, "It was backward when talking about faith, it was backward when talking about going to church." For this reason, strengthening faith for the believers of God and spreading God's salvation in this time period was a great challenge.

VII. Appointments to Office and Ordinations

The needs of the Church for teaching and performing ceremonies such as the Eucharist, baby dedications, baptisms, and marriages were becoming increasingly difficult because of the lack of God's servants. Alternatively, God's servants were not allowed by the government to practice their ministry. Of course, churches in remote areas were more disadvantaged. The ordination of pastors also encountered many obstacles, while in many ministries, only pastors were executed. As the rule of the Church, regarding the blessing and celebration of baptism, only true pastors could celebrate marriages. Therefore, many churches had leaders that were preachers who had to ask pastors who were quite far away to perform the above rituals, so they were always in a passive and inconvenient situation. To conduct the ordination of a minister or a pastor, in addition to the above conditions, it was defined as theological graduation, the grace of the Lord, and the General Confederation's Board approving their serving the church in a particular place. After 1975, they had to be reviewed and approved by the local government at all levels. Therefore, the ordination of a pastor still depended on many issues with which the Church was not proactive, although a missionary was well-deserved in terms of the Church and might have been presented to the government for quite a long time.

Some churches lacked preachers and pastors, so they rarely held a Eucharist. If this situation persisted, the construction of the Church would have faced many obstructions, since there were no trained and inherited clergy. In response to the need in remote areas, the General Confederation sometimes had to enable a volunteer preacher or a prestigious deacon to receive the Eucharist according to need and for a certain period of time.

VIII. Churches in the Highlands

When discussing the crisis after 1975, it is impossible not to mention the work of God in churches in the Highlands regarding ethnic minorities. Suspicions and misunderstandings related to the Fulro (terrorist organization fighting the government) made the Church in the Highlands meet many difficulties. Perhaps someone who belonged to the Fulro also believed in Protestantism, but not all Protestant followers followed Fulro. Moreover, the policy of the CM&A of Vietnam thus far had not been political. However, since 1975, many government officials saw Protestantism and Fulro as always related, even if it was only one, then, it was a threaten agent toward communist authority. Therefore, the activities of most churches in the Central Highlands were suspected and obstructed, and many churches were closed. The connection between the Church's ethnic brothers and the Kinh Church (the Kinh people were also the majority in Vietnam) was not easy. Because of a fear of suspicion and implications, the support for each other was limited or silent. The suspicion was not only of the government but also the Church, and it caused division in the Church. Most believers were not allowed to worship God at the church but had to worship at home. Of course, the authorities did not recognize this case as legal. Nevertheless, thank God, the brothers and sisters kept their faith in accepting all their difficulties in worshiping God.

After the suspicion of the Fulro organization, the Highlands Church had to face suspicions related to the Montagnard Dega Association (MDA). Not only were there suspicions, but the Evangelical Church also came close to being given the name "Dega Evangelical Church." This caused many problems and hindered the activities of the churches in the Highlands, although the Church spoke up and affirmed its position. It must be confirmed that it is completely wrong to call the Vietnamese Evangelical Church the Dega Evangelical Church. There was only an organization called the Montagnard Dega Association, not the "Dega Evangelical Church." This name was actually only used by people who were not knowledgeable or people with prejudices. We will see this point more clearly in the following sections.

IX. House Churches

During this time, obstacles came from without and within. Because of many disagreements about the organization due to discipline or other reasons, some people were no longer in the organization of the Vietnamese Evangelical Church. They had stepped out to form another organization or followed another system or faction. Of course, this was not something new in Church history. What was worth mentioning here was the motivation and consequences of this problem, which caused many misunderstandings and often led to ill-treating the church to strengthen and draw more people to their organizations instead of focusing on preaching the Gospel to save people and encourage new believers. Most of these differences were not about doctrine but about the organization, an issue that must be clarified because otherwise there will be many conflicts between residential groups and CM&A churches. There are even some extremists who have created misunderstandings, digging deep holes in connection with the CM&A Church. Today, regarding denominations, there have too many problems that need to be clearly analyzed to be able to come to an accurate conclusion. In fact, many people still do not know the issues well, making it more difficult for the Church. Concerning the government and those who do not know God, not all are clear about the CM&A, and other Protestant organizations even claim that religion is a superstition, the opiate of society. Therefore, this major problem for the Church concerned Jesus's effort to preach the Gospel and the truth of the Bible while heresy is interfering with the Church.

X. Developmental Delay

Looking at all these issues, no matter how optimistic one was, it was impossible not to worry about the existence and development of the Church, especially those who were down on the Lord's work. In fact, in the first few days after the 1975 event, some thought that the Church would not even survive, let alone develop. Indeed, the Church at that time developed very slowly due to many reasons:

- There were not enough vehicles.
- Finances were inadequate.
- Spirits declined.
- Internal segregation.
- The difficult economic situation of believers.
- Limitations from the government.
- The independence of the Church, not having support as before.
- Changing social circumstances.
- Lack of official training.

Summary

The issues mentioned in relation to the lack of many aspects show the great obstacles of the Church after 1975: psychological issues, material issues, spirituality, organizational problems, and the like. According to a human perspective, these were very big challenges, seemingly impossible to overcome. However, in the view of one with faith in God, one who established and walked in the Church, we are convinced that the Lord will preserve and have a good plan for His Church.

B. The Consolidation

Thank God for His faithfulness, love, and mercy. He taught the Church so much after the 1975 event, so the Church could say, "I will not die, but I will live, recount the work of Jehovah. Jehovah punished me seriously, but not to deliver me to death." (Psalm 118:17-29—NIV)

Indeed, after the event of 1975, everyone's mood was like that of the Israel people when they were exiled. "**1.** By the rivers of Babylon, we sat and wept when we remembered Zion. **2.** There on the poplars, we hung our harps, **3.** for there our captors asked us for songs, our tormentors demanded songs of joy, they said, "Sing us one of the songs of Zion!" **4** How can we sing the songs of the LORD while in a foreign land? (Psalm 137: 1–4).

After a while, the church was aware of God's permission to enter a new stage. It was a sense of God's teaching and an appreciation of what was lost. What God has closed, no one can open, what God opens, no one can close. Where there is a will, there is a way. The church began to get up, relying on God to find a way in His guidance. "Though he may stumble, he will not fall, for the LORD upholds him with his hand" (Psalm 37:24).

It took many years for the Church to regain spirit, settle down, accept reality, and especially depend on God more. Church members needed to be closer to God and equip themselves for spiritual life to face new circumstances and to continue worshiping and serving God.

"Like Habakkuk, the prophet will stand at my watch and station myself on the ramparts, I will look to see what he will say to me" (Hab. 2: 1). Many children of God in the Vietnamese Evangelical Church were also waiting for God's will to reveal what to do and what to avoid in the service of the Lord in this new situation, such as "Trust in the LORD and do good, dwell in the land and enjoy safe pasture." In addition, "Commit your way to the LORD,
trust in him and he will do this. Be still before
the LORD
and wait patiently for him,
do not fret when people succeed in their ways,
when they carry out their wicked schemes." (Psalm 37:3, 5, 7)

The Church now does not have to sit in a place to regret and be pessimistic. Instead, it can stand up, equipped with all that is needed to build and develop the Church. It can strive to bring many people to God in many possible ways within its general limits.

Genesis 41's story about seven years of wealth and seven years of poverty leave us with a very valuable lesson. For people, events may seem unexpected or accidental, but for God, everything happens in His good plan. God has prepared everything and raised the Josephs for the times of need.

I. Training

After 1975, the Holy Bible Institute of Nha Trang also opened for a final school year (1975-1976). After that, the Theology of Nha Trang Institute and the Bible School in Da Lat and Buon Me Thuot were not allowed to operate anymore. Even the training facility was requisitioned by the State. Every year there were fewer than fifty to seventy graduates from the Theological Institute and Bible School who graduated to become pastors and preachers. If they do not continue training, what will the future of the Church be? What will this generation's legacy look like? Thank God, the professors and the pastor, who had silently trained to work with the great missionaries and to serve the Lord, but not to graduate school, were ready in all ways to help them gain every qualification to graduate later. Of course, doing this job was not easy, as it required sacrifices of money and time.

Since there were no schools and facilities, it was necessary to change places regularly to teach and learn. Those who were called by God to do His work were also willing to suffer silently in the study of the word of God. Subsequently, they silently served the churches with the title of volunteer preachers. Despite the difficult circumstances, the Church's need for shepherds was now even worse, not only for the current believers who were lacking leaders, but also for many churches whose new small groups needed the guidance of a servant of God.

The needs were too big, continuous, and systematic while the circumstances and means were too difficult to conduct the training of the Lord's servants. Thank God, where there is a will, there is a way. During the twenty-seven years (1976–2003), from the time when the Theological Institute was deactivated until it was re-established, many servants of God devoted themselves to sacrifice, organizing many training programs silently for those volunteer preachers in any way. What pen can express the ups and downs of training and service that one's predecessors have endured silently during such a long historical era? Thank God, later, when the Church had legal status, more than 600 volunteer preachers were supplemented with theology and validated to formally become preachers or leader pastors by the Church and government.

Before 1975, there were overseas students who were sent to study theology by the General Federation to return to serve the Lord in the work of theological education. After 1975, the Church was no longer allowed because there was no legal status. Because of the need, many children of God studied independently in many different ways, taking advantage of the opportunity to learn God's words and theology. They equipped their spiritual lives with the necessary abilities, to be ready to step into their position when God called and used them. When returning home, although they were not officially serving, students still silently served God while waiting to be officially recognized with their title and office.

In addition to the need to train pastors, preachers, and churches who also needed personnel to serve with much encouragement, development, and evangelization work, the training of personnel was equally important. In the current situation, it is not easy to concentrate and gather a large number of people to participate in certain training programs. Therefore, the Lord's servants in places have trusted the Lord, accepting the difficulty of organizing many training programs both when allowed and silently, because the future of the Church needs both core and peripheral personnel. Whoever has God's grace also has the ability to serve God effectively.

Despite facing difficulties in many aspects, the love and desire for God's children were increasing, so the human resource training programs were actively sought by people in the churches. Many Bible classes of the churches were systematically and regularly organized, even weekly, to meet the needs of the children of God. Even some of the children of God sought opportunities to study the Bible in other churches during the week in addition to studying the Bible in their local churches. Previously, although there were many advantages, few programs were organized, and few people participated. Then, although the need for awareness made tasks more difficult in some respects, many programs were organized and made available for many participants.

For provinces with higher levels of government that empathize with and understand the Church, the Church has gradually sought to organize basic Bible classes, like the previous Primary Bible School for all of God's children in the province. It is not easy to organize Bible classes during the summer season at the small church level, so sometimes, one had to use the word “Bible Revision class” to be allowed to organize. When the speaker came to participate, the appropriate words had to be used, for example, “sharing,” not the word “preaching.” Thus, in any form, “Necessity is the mother of invention,” and the Church tried to organize the programs that were needed to prepare successors in many of the current and future Church services.

Thank God! Through these training activities, the Church of God in the period of crisis stood strong, continuing to build and develop. The Church does not “sleep under the juniper tree.” Instead, it now rises up to “eat and drink, and then get the strength of that food” (1 Kings 19: 5–10) that continues the things God wants. Although the Bible, books, and documents were hardly there, by the enlightenment of the Holy Spirit, the word of God became alive and sweet, deeply profound for the children of God at that time.

Another important issue was Sunday School. Because it was related to the "school" issue, when wanting to organize a Sunday School class, the Church had to ask permission. Therefore, Sunday School was renamed “Sunday Bible Study” or “Weekly Bible Lesson.” Since there were few resources like before, many churches had to re-learn the old materials, or the head pastors had to find appropriate materials or write them themselves. Thus, the faith of the faithful was built and raised.

II. Missionary Work

The second important factor was missionary work. This is God's command, so the Church must do it at any cost. However, what should the church do between the current ties? According to State regulations, the Gospel was only preached in the Church. While religious freedom was respected, the Church was also bound by non-religious freedoms. Consequently, missionary work, preaching events, and preaching campaigns were no longer allowed to perform as before. So, what should the Church do? This was a great challenge to the execution of what Jesus commanded before returning to Heaven: "Go and preach the good news to everyone in the world" (Mark 16:15).

By the grace of God and the willingness to accept all difficulties to obey God's command, the Church always took the opportunity to bring salvation to all, from weekly preaching programs to individual devotions. In addition to regularly organizing programs, the church also held special preaching programs. This was something new and unprecedented in the period before 1975. Even the churches in the countryside did not have the means as in the city to organize a monthly preaching program on Sunday nights falling on the full moon.

Personal preaching methods were still applied thoroughly at every opportunity, even though the situation was more problematic than ever before, it was still very effective in this period. After the preaching, the children of God continued to invite friends to church to listen to the Gospel. By the work of the Holy Spirit, the evangelistic events at churches achieved many results. Thank God, inviting friends to come to a church to listen to the Gospel was quite easy because of friends' desire. Even those who were previously very difficult to invite to the church now had soft hearts to receive the Lord. After that, they became the staff who served very effectively at evangelistic events. Therefore, many more people were saved. Many lives were miraculously transformed by God and became very effective living lectures.

In addition, servants and children of God also took advantage of opportunities such as funerals, wedding ceremonies, and believers' birthdays to evangelize guests who were friends. The slogan "All for those who have not been saved" was followed thoroughly. Media such as tapes and discs introduced God, including evangelistic lectures to friends, so they can hear preaching about the salvation of God at home.

There were times when no preaching events were organized in churches. Instead, the servants and children of God organized a tour. Tourists invited many friends to join in, to have the opportunity to preach to them, even preaching in cars from the time a car departed to when it reached the tourism destination. Public social charity was also a favorable environment to introduce God. Sometimes, because of great distances, when children of God could not invite friends to hear the Gospel, the children of God would use mobile phones to connect one to another so their friends could listen to the Word of God clearly, even when sitting at evangelistic meetings. In this era, the love for God and the lost souls of believers was so unspeakably touching. In short, many methods were used to save people for God, even though it took much effort or money to surmount difficulties.

The Ethnic People

Dân tộc	chưa từng nghe về đạo Chúa (%)	Đã nghe nhưng chưa tin (%)	Đã nghe và tin (%)
Bana	36	56	8
Bố Y	91	9	0
Brâu	19	67	14
Bru-Vân Kiều	55	41	4
Chăm	81	18	1
Chơro	19	65	16
Churu	9	71	20
Chứt	94	6	0
Co	61	35	4
Cơlau	88	12	0
Công	92	8	0
Dao	78	21	1
Êđê	0	51	49
Giarai	15	58	27
Giáy	85	15	0
Gié Triêng	5	65	30
Hà Nhì	86	14	0
H'Mông	16	62	22
Hoa	36	59	5
H'Rê	71	27	2

Katu	75	24	1
Kháng	97	3	0
Khmer	84	15	1
Khmu	83	16	1

Among 54 Vietnamese ethnic groups, up to the year 2001, Christianity was transmitted to most areas of Vietnam. The people who responded positively to Christianity were K "Ho, Ede, and M'nong.

K'ho	0	50	50
Laha	98	2	0
Lahủ	83	17	0
Lào	95	5	0
La Chi	93	7	0
Lôlô	97	3	0
Lự	97	3	0
Mạ	26	58	16
Mảng	98	2	0
Mnông	6	47	47
Mường	79	20	1
Ngái	94	6	0
Nùng	90	9	1
Ơđu	100	0	0
Pà Thẻn	92	8	0
Phù Lá	84	15	1
Pu Péo	95	5	0
Raglay	35	61	4
Rơmăm	84	16	0

Sán chay	90	10	0
Sán Dìu	68	31	1
Sila	99	1	0
Tà Ôi	79	20	1
Tày	90	9	1
Thái	86	13	1
Thổ	77	23	0
Việt	40	51	9
Xinh Mun	96	4	0
Xê Đăng	46	49	5

III. Prayer Spirit

Yet another factor related to the consolidation and development of the Church in this period was the spirit of prayer. Previously, the Church did not truly trust God because it had so many opportunities. When these were no more, the Church just only knew to trust in God, with a more earnest spirit of prayer. Most churches opened doors to pray every morning to know God's will, learn, and fellowship with God and each other. The Church was closer to God than ever. Members would repent, pray for God to visit and teach the right things to do and the things to avoid for the Church to grow unscathed in its new phases. At that time, the Church had almost no relationship with foreign churches. The Church had to stand on their own feet completely, while meeting many deadlocks, be they financial, facilities, means, etc. Accordingly, the church at that time could be described as the mood of David in Psalm 61: 1–4.

1. For the music director, on string instrument, of David.
2. Hear my cry, O God, listen to my prayer.
3. From the end of the earth I call to You when my heart is faint.
Lead me to the rock that is higher than I.
4. For You have been a refuge for me, a tower of strength before the enemy."

Thank God, the Vietnamese Evangelical Church experienced the spiritual energy of prayer. Thanks to that, the Church was strong enough to overcome all circumstances, to "not only believing in Christ alone, suffering for Him more" (Philippians 1:29). Because believing that God's will is good, fully, the Church lives and always serves the Lord, everywhere in the spirit of peace. God does not just save the people who belong to Him from the fiery furnace, He also saves them in the furnace fire.

IV. Bible and Christian Literature

The Bible and Christian literature were very scarce after 1975, but because the needs of God's people were too great, the Church had to find ways to meet this demand. When the Bible and hymnals were no longer printed, the existence of Bibles, hymns, and religion was even more precious. Then, the headquarters of the Bible Society, on Suong Nguyet Anh Street, had a few remaining Bibles. People with organizational responsibilities had to find ways to distribute drips and drops of the Bible in some difficult, sometimes unreasonable conditions to extend its distribution for fairness. After a short time, there were no Bibles for distribution, even in the Christian reading room.

Like waiting for sunshine after a long time in the rain, in the 1980s, the Evangelical churches, both South–North, received gifts from the East and West German Evangelical Church consisting of 20,000 sets of Bibles and hymns. Thank God! However, some were lost. People even found some of the Bible used to make wrapping paper, meaning that, for many children of God, there was not enough Bible to use. Nonetheless, the Bible was a great joy to people in those times.

Thus, the long sunshine had only a little rain, it was not permanent. Understanding the needs of the people in Vietnam, believers from other countries sometimes got the opportunity to return to Vietnam, trying to bring the Bible back to believers. Because it was too necessary for believers, some people patiently wrote or photocopied the Bible. However, all these measures could not respond to the Church's great needs back then, let alone the future. Therefore, the servants and children of God silently used the simplest and most discreet printing possible to have a large number of Bibles and hymns for Christians. There were drawbacks. The quality of printing was not high, the Bible was double-sized, heavy, and inconvenient to bring to church. Moreover, this illegal work faced many obstacles. Nevertheless, God's children were very happy to have the Bible and hymns to use in their worship of God to learn His words.

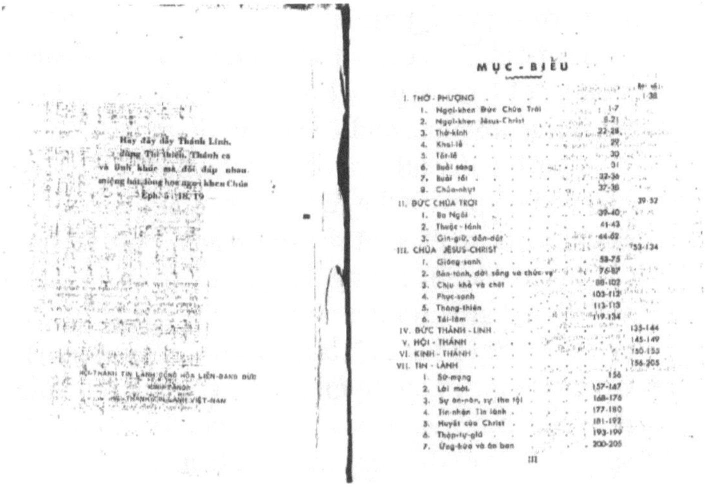

Hãy đầy dẫy Thánh Linh,
dùng Thi thiên, Thánh ca
và Bài khúc mà đối đáp nhau
miệng hát lòng họa ngợi khen Chúa
Eph. 5 : 18, 19

HỘI-THÁNH TIN LÀNH CỘNG HÒA LIÊN-BANG ĐỨC

MỤC - BIỂU

III

Hymns Given from Germany

There were some special cases. Christians abroad have Bible but they never read where Vietnamese Christians back in Vietnam were thrilled to have Bible to read. There were also the cases when they brought a large number, which were confiscated by the government. Overall, at every step, God has opened the way to the need for Bibles, and there was a gradual response. Since the 1990s, the government had a more open policy, so Bibles and hymns were officially allowed to print to respond to the reasonable needs of the Church. Truly, after 1975, this was a special milestone that brought joy to the Church after a long time of anticipation.

Later, the Church had more other Vietnamese Bible translations such as the implied version and modern version, besides the traditional 1926 translation. This enriched resources for the Bible studies of Christians who for a long time lacked the Bible, hymns, and Christian literature. Before being officially allowed to print, church leaders had come up with the idea to print biblical documents in a secret facility that we would have hymns to use for a long time. Moreover, in the 1990s, the government allowed the hymns to be printed. City Music Publisher chose South East County to print the hymns. The content remained the same but was rearranged to correct a few spelling errors and use thinner, leaner paper. Accordingly, after obtaining legal status, the Church needed the permission to print hymns again. The government forced the Church to delete two songs, everyone needed Rescue on page 354 and Who Gives Good News on page 361, because some words were unacceptable with their misunderstood meanings. The Church did not agree to delete these two songs, the Church only wanted to edit them.

Apart from the need for the Bible and the hymns, the Church had a great demand for Christian literature, such as spiritual books, Bible preaching, and Sunday School lessons. Accordingly, there were many books that needed reprinting. New books were needed for popularization, but it was still very difficult to request permission to print books for spirituality or other materials besides the Bible, including hymns. Thus, the Church silently looked for opportunity to print out Christian resources who those who needed.

With very limited means and no license, it was difficult to print documents for the Church. Even so, churches in some places also had temporary articles and documents to learn God's words, even though they might have been incomplete. Regarding new documents, after 1975, when the Christian bookroom was no longer active, there were no books compiled and released. Occasionally, new Christian books were received that were very precious, so every way was found to copy them secretly to popularize them. However, their number was limited, not abundant and rich like before. Consequently, God's children and servants, especially those responsible for publicizing God's word to feed the sheep, had to invest more time, seek messages from the Lord, rely on the Holy Spirit, and thank God rather than searching for books. Thanks to that, the church still received fresh, vivid messages from the word of God preached by the Lord's servants and experiences with God.

On the contrary, since the books were popular, there were benefits and disadvantages, because books were not only coming from righteous sources. This was when wrong teachings went to the Church, harming or losing the faith of some Christians. During the opening of Vietnam's economy, the Church was also faced with both sides when many evil factions intervened with the

Church, besides the support of Christians coming from abroad.

V. Reconstruction of the Church

Thank God, even though there were many limitations in the construction and development of the Church, there were still many people to be saved. Consequently, most churches did not have enough room for believers to worship God and conduct other activities. Moreover, most churches had been built for many years, so it was a downgrade to rebuild. Because it was impossible to build a church. The church resolved the problem by dividing itself many times to worship on Sunday or finding ways to temporarily expand the church to make room for God's children to live.

Since the 1990s, the government allowed many churches and facilities to rebuild. The big problem was finances, because donations were limited. Thank God, He knew the needs of the Church. Many individuals or Christian organizations were touched to help to build a convenient and spacious church, which brought joy to God's people. We could not name every benefactor, but we could recognize some organizations, such as the ICM Association (International Cooperating Ministries), the Korean Welfare Association, and Korean churches. They encouraged many believers in the country to help build, renovate, or expand many Evangelical churches in Vietnam. Most were touched by the love for God and the dedicated spirit of the Christians in South Korea and other countries for God's work in Vietnam.

Tien Thuy Church (Ben Tre) Old and New

VI. Organization

As stated in the "crisis" section, after 1975, there were many disturbances in the organization of the Church, from the General Federation to the church branches. Gradually, the Church was stable with new circumstances, depending on individual church resources, and it started planning. The Church relies on its God to serve God, not to hang like the Israel people who came to Babylon. Thank God, the Church used its own resources to continue the work that God gave it, though it was aware of itself as the "poorest and smallest," with a great many challenges and obstacles. It was still reassuring because God said, "I will be with you" (Judges 6: 14–16). Although "The storm was so great that the waves were covered with boats," the Church still believed there was God in the boat. Even though "He is sleeping," when the time of need arose, "He got up, rebuked the wind and the sea, then quietly like sheets" (Matthew 8: 24-26)., Thus, the faith of God's children at this time was strengthened to shape and develop the Church.

The Church's branches tried to organize many programs to meet Christians' needs. The fellowship of the Church had long been deadlocked. Now, real events were the foundation of programs like devotions, Thanksgiving, the anniversary of the founding of the Church, dedications of the new churches, etc. Such opportunities were a chance for the children of

God to attend, fellowship, and listen to the word of God. The Church was very excited, because there were many people at their programs, like previous County Councils.

Subsequently, the churches in the provinces and cities organized prayer and devotional events every year or every quarter. From this period onward, the spirit of fellowship among the Church members was more vibrant, and the relationship between the church branches with the General Federation was better, more regular, and more effective.

VII. Government Innovation

Since the 1990s, the government had some policy changes. It was more open to religion (but not all). Moreover, some government officials understood the Gospel more than before, so organizing some activities of the Church became relatively easier. Under the Constitution, the State regulated the freedom of belief and religion, but it needed clear explanations through legal documents. Previously, there were decrees from the time of military management (after 1975), needed for suitable amendments. In recent times, because of innovations and to be more appropriate for the times, the State has published decrees, circulars, guidance, document explanations, etc., for the government to clarify the State's policy on religion. Accordingly, the activities of the Church after this were relatively open because there were specific rules. If, however, a local law was not properly implemented, it caused many issues for God's work. In 2005, the new Ordinance on Religious Belief Life helped expand Gospel activity.

PART VII

Between 2001–2011

FROM LEGAL STATUS TO THE PRESENT DAY

I. Establishment of an Advocacy Committee

II. Drafting Committee of the Charter

III. Preparing for the General Council

IV. Legal Status

V. Acknowledging the Pastor's Office

VI. Pastor Pham Xuan Thieu Returns to God

VII. Difficulties

VIII. Re-establishing the Theological Institute

IX. The 44th Meeting of the General Assembly

X. Publishing the Pastoral Newsletter

XI. Preaching Gospel outside the Church

XII. The 45th Meeting of the General Assembly

XIII. Reunification Issue

Part VII

An important milestone of the Vietnamese Evangelical Church (South) was recognition as a legal organization of the Socialist Republic of Vietnam. According to the hundred-year history of the Vietnamese Protestant Church, the Church has survived many political changes and has been legally recognized three times: the first time in 1942 by the Governor-General of Indochina, the second time in 1952 by the Republic of Vietnam, and the third time in 2001 by the Socialist Republic of Vietnam. To clarify this issue, since the country divided in 1954, the Vietnamese Evangelical Church was also divided into two organizations. In the North, in 1955, the deacons and pastors organized the General Assembly to elect a Board of Management of the Northern Federation Church Assembly, revising the charter to submit to the Government of the Democratic Republic of Vietnam. It had new legal status until 1963. To the South, since 1954, the Church continued to operate normally under the regime of the Vietnam Republic from the 17th parallel to Ca Mau until today.

Since 1975, the Vietnamese Evangelical Church (South) has operated normally but has not yet been legally accredited by the government because the Church has not been considered legal, favorable conditions were not created, as they were for other religions. Therefore, it was not easy to fulfill the desires of the Church in building and developing as it should have. Consequently, one of the problems the Church cared about was legal recognition and conditions. This lasted a quarter of a century. Servants and children of God had to wait in weariness, though they thought that, when they had legal status it would be better than the present. In fact, many times God's children and servants found many ways to encourage internal resources as well as contact the government to find direction for the Church from the current Government. This was like winning back justice in the history of the Church. Once Christianity was recognized as legitimate under the Roman Empire, Christianity made a "place under the sun." Many documents were sent to the government. A tactical committee was also established, but it was useless.

I. Establishment of Advocacy Committee

When elected to the position of head leader of the Vietnamese Evangelical Church (South), Pastor Ong Van Huyen said to delegates in the 42nd meeting of the General Assembly Federation in 1976: "I am just a night watcher waiting for the morning to hand it over to another one." He was a "night watcher" who had to wait for 23 years. Even though he passed away, the Church still was not allowed to organize the General Council.

In 2000, most members of the Board of Management of the General Federation, including both the head leader and vice leader, had passed away (Pastor Doan Van Mieng, vice-leader, rested in peace with God on December 19, 1994, and Pastor Ong Van Huyen, the head leader, rested in peace with God on July 26, 1999). An Advocacy Committee was established to prepare for the Meeting of the General Assembly Federation and the process to apply for legal recognition.

The first step of the process to select personnel to form an Advocacy Committee approved by the government required much time. Who could be chosen? Which standard? Did the government or the church choose? Finally, the list was submitted to 25 candidates: Pastor Duong Thanh, Pastor Ngo Van Buu, Pastor Tran Ba Thanh, Section Prof. Dinh Thong, Pastor Huynh Thien Buu, Pastor Phan Quang Thieu, Pastor Ngo Thai Binh, Pastor Ksor Brao, Pastor Ha Brong, Pastor Le Khac Cung, Pastor Luu Van Pastor, Pastor Tang Van Hi, Pastor Le Van Hoa, Pastor Le Khac Hoa, Pastor Le Hoang Long, Pastor Nguyen Van Na, Pastor Bui Trung Nguon, Pastor Pham Xuan Thieu, Pastor Nguyen Trung Thong, Pastor Ma Phuc Tin, Section Monk Thai Phuoc Truong, Pastor Nguyen Van Thanh Van, Pastor Nguyen Huu Vien, Pastor Nguyen Xuan Vong, and Pastor Tran Luong Y.

A list of advocacy boards was approved by the government (Document No. 378 TB / TGCP, October 13, 2000). On October 21, 2000, Saigon Evangelical Church solemnly celebrated the approval of the Committee for Religious Affairs for Personnel of Advocacy of the Vietnamese Evangelical Church (South). When listening to the announcement, most of God's servants and children were happy and excited. Many people, though, realized that this was just the first step to attain legal status.

HỘI THÁNH TIN LÀNH VIỆT NAM (MIỀN NAM)
VĂN PHÒNG TỔNG LIÊN HỘI
155, Trần Hưng Đạo — Quận 1,
TP. HỒ CHÍ MINH

Điện thoại: [illegible]

Số 444 /TLH/[illegible]

[illegible]

TP. Hồ Chí Minh, ngày 26 tháng 12 năm 1994

Kính gửi :

- BAN TRỊ SỰ TỔNG LIÊN HỘI - HTTLVNMN
- CHỦ NHIỆM VÀ BAN TRỊ SỰ CÁC ĐỊA HẠT:
  - ☐ Trung Trung Bộ (Đà Nẵng)
  - ☐ Nam Trung Bộ (Nha Trang)
  - ☐ Đông Nam Bộ (TP.HCM)
  - ☐ Trung Nam Bộ (Vĩnh Long)
  - ☐ Tây Nam Bộ (Cần Thơ)

Trích yếu V/v. THƯ ỦY NHIỆM

Để gìn giữ tốt đẹp công việc chung nhà Chúa và sự hiệp một giữa vòng anh em, cũng để đề phòng những việc đáng tiếc có thể xảy ra sau khi tôi qua đời, với tư cách là Hội Trưởng Hội Thánh Tin Lành Việt Nam miền Nam, tôi ủy nhiệm :

I/- Ông Mục sư DƯƠNG THANH, Quyền Chủ nhiệm Địa hạt Trung Trung Bộ thay tôi (đúng theo tinh thần tổ chức và điều lệ của HTTLVNMN) chịu trách nhiệm triệu tập toàn thể Ban Trị sự Tổng Liên Hội, gồm 05 vị sau đây :

1- Ông MS. Trần Bá Thành, Quyền Chủ nhiệm ĐH Đông Nam Bộ.
2- Ông MS. Ngô Văn Bửu, Quyền Chủ nhiệm ĐH.Trung Nam Bộ.
3- Ông MS. Đinh Thường, Quyền Chủ nhiệm ĐH. Nam trung Bộ.
4- Cụ MS. Nguyễn Xuân Vọng, Nghị viên Tổng Liên Hội.
5- Ông MS. Tăng Văn Hi, Nghị viên Tổng Liên Hội.

họp tại trụ sở Tổng Liên Hội số 155, Trần Hưng Đạo, Q1, TP.HCM để đề cử bầu phiếu kín các chức vụ :

A. Quyền HỘI TRƯỞNG Hội Thánh Tin Lành Việt Nam miền Nam.
B. Quyền TỔNG THƯ KÝ Ban Trị sự Tổng Liên Hội.
C. Quyền TỔNG THỦ QUỸ Ban Trị sự Tổng Liên Hội.

để tiếp tục điều hành công việc nhà Chúa chung của Hội Thánh Tin Lành Việt Nam miền Nam.

II. Thư ủy nhiệm này chỉ có giá trị thi hành khi tôi về nước Chúa.

III. Tôi ủy quyền cho Ông Mục sư Đặng Thiên Ân, Chánh Văn phòng Tổng Liên Hội chịu trách nhiệm chỉ công bố văn thư này sau khi tôi qua đời./-

HỘI TRƯỞNG

Mục sư [illegible]

After the ceremony, there were many things the Committee must do. On the one hand, the Church must interact with the authorities to update the church's activities as their requirement, thus, church's leader organized many meetings with believers in the Church to advocate for and explain the steps to attain legal status for the Church. There were many little-known tasks in this process. Believers were listened to, as was the government. Tradition was important, including the Church's charter, however, the government disagreed with many believers and God's servants. Otherwise, the government proposal might be considered as unacceptable, no progress, anti-government, and unwise. Alternatively, they would be considered state-owned, not standing with God and the Church.

Because of the limits of the book *The Secret Truth behind the Stage*, this period cannot be shown in detail. Hopefully, we can mention it in the future.

HỘI THÁNH TIN LÀNH VIỆT NAM (MIỀN NAM)
VĂN PHÒNG TỔNG LIÊN HỘI
155 Trần Hưng Đạo - Quận 1
TP. Hồ Chí Minh
Điện thoại: 8340586
Số: 32/TLH.VP

CỘNG HÒA XÃ HỘI CHỦ NGHĨA VIỆT NAM
Độc Lập - Tự Do - Hạnh Phúc

TP. HCM, ngày 24 tháng 8 năm 2000

ĐƠN ĐỀ NGHỊ

V/v.- Thành lập Ban Vận động Đại hội đồng
Hội thánh Tin Lành Việt Nam (miền Nam).

Kính gửi: THỦ TƯỚNG CHÍNH PHỦ
NƯỚC CỘNG HÒA XÃ HỘI CHỦ NGHĨA VIỆT NAM
Đồng Kính gửi: - BAN TÔN GIÁO CỦA CHÍNH PHỦ
- ỦY BAN NHÂN DÂN TP. HỒ CHÍ MINH.

Thay mặt toàn thể tín hữu Hội thánh Tin Lành Việt Nam (miền Nam), chúng tôi kính gửi đến Thủ tướng Chính phủ lời chào thăm và cầu chúc tốt đẹp nhất.

Kính thưa Thủ tướng,

- Được sự quan tâm và sự hướng dẫn của Nhà nước.

- Theo thư ủy nhiệm số 144/TLH/VP. ngày 26-12-1994 của Cụ cố Mục sư Ông Văn Huyên, Hội trưởng Hội thánh Tin Lành Việt Nam miền Nam.

Chúng tôi gồm 6 Mục sư có tên trong thư ủy nhiệm nói trên nhóm họp tại TP Hồ Chí Minh ngày 24-8-2000 đã thống nhất:

Trân trọng kính xin Thủ tướng Chính phủ xem xét cho chúng tôi:

1.- Thành lập Ban Vận động để tiến tới Đại hội đồng Hội thánh Tin Lành Việt Nam miền Nam, hoàn chỉnh tư cách pháp nhân của Hội thánh và xây dựng đường hướng hoạt động mới của Giáo hội theo tinh thần đồng hành với dân tộc và hoạt động tuân thủ chính sách, pháp luật của Nhà nước.

2.- Kính trình danh sách Ban Vận động gồm 25 Mục sư tiêu biểu với các chức danh cụ thể (Có danh sách kèm theo).

3.- Cho phép Ban Vận động làm việc tại Văn phòng Tổng Liên Hội, số 155 Trần Hưng Đạo, Q.1, TP Hồ Chí Minh.

Kính mong Thủ tướng Chính phủ và Ban Tôn giáo của Chính phủ chấp thuận nguyện vọng của Hội thánh Tin Lành Việt Nam miền Nam.

Xin chân thành cám ơn Thủ tướng.

Xin Chúa ban phước lành cho Thủ tướng.

Chúng tôi đồng ký tên,

Mục sư DƯƠNG THÀNH — Mục sư NGÔ VĂN BỬU — Mục sư ĐINH THỐNG

Mục sư TRẦN BÁ THÀNH — Mục sư NGUYỄN XUÂN VỌNG — Mục sư TĂNG VĂN HI

BAN TÔN GIÁO CỦA CHÍNH PHỦ

DANH SÁCH
BAN VẬN ĐỘNG HỘI THÁNH TIN LÀNH VIỆT NAM(MIỀN NAM).
(Đính kèm Thông báo số 378 TB/TGCP, ngày 13 tháng 10 năm 2000)

TT	Họ và tên	năm sinh	Nơi cư trú	Chức danh BVĐ
1	Mục sư Dương Thạnh	1935	Đà Nẵng	Trưởng ban
2	Mục sư Ngô Văn Bửu	1940	Đồng Tháp	Phó Trưởng Ban
3	Mục sư Trần Bá Thành	1935	TP Hồ Chí Minh	Phó Trưởng Ban
4	Mục sư Đinh Thống	1931	Phú Yên	Phó TrưởngBan
5	Mục sư Huỳnh Thiên Bửu	1951	TP Hồ Chí Minh	Uỷ viên
6	Mục sư Phan Quang Thiệu	1947	TP Hồ Chí Minh	Uỷ viên
7	Mục sư Ngô Thái Bình	1936	Đà Nẵng	Uỷ viên
8	Mục sư K'sor Brao	1939	Gia Lai	Uỷ viên
9	Mục sư Ha Broug	1922	Lâm Đồng	Uỷ viên
10	Mục sư Lê Khắc Cung	1926	Đắc Lắc	Uỷ viên
11	Mục sư Lưu Văn Giáo	1943	Khánh Hoà	Uỷ viên
12	Mục sư Tăng Văn Hy	1942	Bến Tre	Uỷ viên
13	Mục sư Lê Văn Hòa	1949	Sóc Trăng	Uỷ viên
14	Mục sư Lê Khắc Hóa	1940	Bình Thuận	Uỷ viên
15	Mục sư Lê Hoàng Long	1943	Cần Thơ	Uỷ viên
16	Mục sư Nguyễn Văn Na	1945	Đà nẵng	Uỷ viên
17	Mục sư Bùi Trung Nguơn	1944	TP Hồ Chí Minh	Uỷ viên
18	Mục sư Phạm Xuân Thiều	1944	Khánh Hoà	Uỷ viên
19	Mục sư Nguyễn Trung Thông	1952	Vĩnh Long	Uỷ viên
20	Mục sư Mã Phúc Tín	1939	Quảng Nam	Uỷ viên
21	Mục sư Thái Phước Trường	1953	TP Hồ Chí Minh	Uỷ viên
22	M.S. Nguyễn Văn Thanh Vân	1939	Tiền Giang	Uỷ viên
23	Mục sư Nguyễn Hữu Viễn	1942	Đồng Nai	Uỷ viên
24	Mục sư nguyễn Xuân Vọng	1916	Quảng Nam	Uỷ viên
25	Mục sư Trần Lương Y	1931	Long An	Uỷ viên

Tổng số: 25 vị mục sư trong Ban Vận động Hội thánh Tin lành Việt Nam(MN).

HỘI THÁNH TIN LÀNH VIỆT NAM (MIỀN NAM)
BAN VẬN ĐỘNG ĐẠI HỘI ĐỒNG TỔNG LIÊN HỘI LẦN THỨ 43

CỘNG HÒA XÃ HỘI CHỦ NGHĨA VIỆT NAM
Độc lập - Tự Do - Hạnh phúc

TP. Hồ Chí Minh, ngày 21-10-2000

LỜI KÊU GỌI

CỦA BAN VẬN ĐỘNG TIẾN TỚI ĐẠI HỘI ĐỒNG TỔNG LIÊN HỘI LẦN THỨ 43
HOÀN CHỈNH TƯ CÁCH PHÁP NHÂN HỘI THÁNH TIN LÀNH VIỆT NAM MIỀN NAM

Kính gởi: - QUÍ CỤ MỤC SƯ, TRUYỀN ĐẠO TRÍ SỰ
- QUÍ QUẢ PHỤ MỤC SƯ, TRUYỀN ĐẠO
- QUÍ MỤC SƯ, TRUYỀN ĐẠO
và QUÍ TÍN HỮU Hội thánh Tin Lành Việt Nam (miền Nam)

Trước hết, chúng tôi xin thân ái gởi đến Quí vị lời chào thăm trong tình yêu Cứu Chúa Jesus Christ.
Thưa quí vị,

Thể theo nguyện vọng của toàn thể Mục sư, Truyền Đạo và tín hữu trong Hội thánh Tin Lành Việt Nam (miền Nam), được Mục sư Hội trưởng Ông Văn Huyên có Thư Ủy nhiệm ngày 26-12-1994 uỷ nhiệm việc điều hành Hội thánh cho các Mục sư : Dương Thạnh, Trần Bá Thành, Ngô Văn Bửu, Đinh Thống, Nguyễn Xuân Vọng và Tăng Văn Hi. Ngày 24-8-2000, chúng tôi đã trình đơn đề nghị lên Thủ tướng Chính phủ xin phép thành lập Ban Vận động tiến tới Đại Hội đồng Tổng Liên Hội lần thứ 43, hoàn chỉnh tư cách pháp nhân Hội thánh Tin Lành Việt Nam (miền Nam).

Được ủy quyền của Thủ tướng Chính phủ, ngày 13-10-2000 công văn số 378-TB/TGCP. Ban Tôn Giáo của Chính Phủ đã chấp thuận nhân sự Ban Vận Động của Hội thánh Tin Lành Việt Nam (miền Nam).

Đây là tin vui lớn đầu tiên trong quá trình tiến tới Đại Hội đồng Tổng Liên Hội lần thứ 43, nhằm hoàn chỉnh tư cách pháp nhân, mở trang sử mới cho Hội thánh Tin Lành Việt Nam (miền Nam).

Ban Vận Động kêu gọi toàn thể Quí tôi con của Chúa thiết tha cầu nguyện xin Đức Chúa Trời điều hướng cho Đại Hội Đồng Tổng Liên Hội lần thứ 43 lịch sử nầy sẽ được diễn ra trong sự quan phòng của Chúa.

Cầu mong Quí vị quan tâm, đóng góp tích cực vào việc hoàn chỉnh hiến chương sao cho phát huy được truyền thống tốt đẹp của Hội thánh Tin Lành Việt Nam (miền Nam), tôn trọng truyền thống dân tộc và đời sống xã hội, phù hợp với chính sách và pháp luật.

Vì sự thiêng liêng cao quí và tốt đẹp của Hội Thánh, mong Quí vị hãy bầu chọn những đại biểu xứng đáng đại diện cho chi hội của mình để dự Đại Hội đồng. Qua đó, tiếp tục bầu chọn những Mục sư, Truyền Đạo, tín hữu có đức hạnh về Đạo, đời, ơn Chúa vào Ban Trị sự Tổng Liên Hội thánh Tin Lành Việt Nam (miền Nam).

Theo lời Chúa dạy, mỗi chúng ta đều là chi thể trong thân thể Chúa, và là muối của đất. như lời khuyên của Cụ cố Mục sư Hội Trưởng: "Một tín hữu tốt phải là một công dân tốt".

Vì Chúa, vì đất nước, vì dân tộc và tổ quốc, chúng ta hãy đồng lòng hiệp một trong Đức Thánh Linh, phát huy tôn chỉ và mục đích của Tin Lành Việt Nam, và luôn gắn bó với dân tộc.

Xin Chúa ban phước lành dư dật trên toàn thể Quí vị.

BAN VẬN ĐỘNG

II. Committee Charter

An important task in this period was to send out a drafting committee for the charter, includi8ng rules for submission. One of the conditions to be considered for legal status is the passage of a must-have charter government. Before 1975, in addition to the current charter, the Church repeatedly drafted an amended charter, but it was not approved by the General Council, so the old charter was still valid in the Church. For this reason, it needed to be edited appropriately, especially in the country's new context.

The drafting committee of the Charter included members: Pastor Ngo Van Buu, Head of Committee, Pastor Pham Xuan Thieu, vice-committee leader, Pastor Phan Quang Thieu, Pastor Tran, Ba Thanh, Pastor Le Van Thien, Pastor Le Cao Quy, Pastor Khau Anh Tuan,

Pastor Huynh Thien Buu, Preacher Nguyen Kim Thach, Ms. Ngo Thi Hong An, and Mr. Nguyen Van Thanh. The Vietnamese Evangelical Church met forty-two times. Often, the charter was compiled, amended, and approved, including rules to be the foundation for the operation of the organizational system of the Church in different social contexts.

The new charter was drafted based on previous rules. It consisted of ten chapters with seventy-nine rules. Of course, there were some changes compared to the old rules that must be discussed with the functional departments several times before approval by the government and the General Assembly of Federation Vietnamese Churches.

The most important and influential change to the organization's life and development of the Church was the county system mechanism. This was over and above Church expectation because the government did not allow. Therefore, according to the new charter, instead of a three-level system as before, the Church mechanism only had two levels, which was the General Federation churches and the churches. Heretofore, when there was a county mechanism, two-thirds of the churchwork was done by the board management of the county, but when following the new charter, not all issues were resolved that the Church submitted to the General Federation of Churches. Surely, the board management of the

General Federation would be busier, and it would take longer to resolve problems, especially when the church was getting bigger.

The second change was adding "the Church Council mechanism" to the charter, which was never before included in the charter of the Church in Vietnam or other countries. Because this was a new mechanism, few people understand it. Instead of supportive, this mechanism has brought many difficulties to the administration of the General Federation, causing many problems between the Board Management of Federation churches and the Church Council. It created conflict and divided the clergy. The problem was not the mechanism, but humans. I nstead of supporting the Board Management of the Federation, the church council always sought opposition, wanting mastery instead of paying attention to the quality of the church dignitaries. They also wanted to supervise the management of both Federation churches and the churches. This created a "trampled on" effect in the organization of the Church. This was a great lesson for the Church, when rules and the charter were changed and applied. In addition, many people thought they had to add a charter in some places or mechanisms from another country. However, depending on the state and circumstances of our Church, we must understand how to apply rules in the right way and at the appropriate time to have effective results. We must not forget the lesson of God's people in the old days, quitting a theocracy to switch to a democracy (humanity), just because we are imitating other countries with kings.

III. Preparing for the General Council Meeting

One of the most important tasks in moving towards legal status was a leader board (General Federation of Churches), which was approved, with an approved charter by the government. As mentioned, the new charter was inherited from an old charter of the Church. However, the government did not approve the new charter, so it was not possible to organize a meeting of the General Council. To be enforceable, the charter had to be approved by General Assembly after it was drafted and was approved by the government. Accordingly, the second step was to be prepared for the meeting of the General Council of the Federation Churches. But to organize the meeting required much discussion, so the Advocacy Committee meetings were held several times to quickly conduct the meeting of the General Council. However, during discussions, many issues were not simple and easy because they related to the tradition of the Church and the permission of the government.

Some specific issues should be mentioned as follows:

- According to the continuation of history, this meeting of the General Assembly is the 43rd

General Council, but the government forced the Church to call this the first meeting of the General Council. For the government, after 1975, this was the first time that the Vietnamese Evangelical Church (South) held the conference, but the Church believed it had been established since 1911 and had its 42nd council meeting. Hence, it had not been established recently. If the government called this the first meeting, the Advocacy Committee could not agree to organize. If not for the first General Council, the government would not have allowed the organization. After many discussions, in the end, the solution was acceptable it was the first General Meeting (43rd according to history of the Evangelical Church).

- The Advocacy Committee also had disagreements about the time to organize and the duration of the organization. About the time duration, some said that it should be held urgently; others did not agree, because they were not ready to prepare. It was Christmas and the Lunar New Year. In terms of time, some people thought that there was no need for many days; only a few days were enough. In addition, the approval of the Charter was simple, and the election to the Board Management of General Federation was fast, because they only chose 23 persons among the 25 candidates of the Advocacy Committee. But some persons on the advocacy committee did not agree because much preparation was needed for essential steps related to the General Assembly. Finally, the Advocacy Committee voted to organize the first Conference of the General Council (43rd according to Church history) February 7–9, 2001, at the Saigon Evangelical Church, which was accepted by authorities. This was a history board for the later 25 years (1976 to 2001), so we could hold the General Council Conference of Federation churches.

- Election procedure issues were also discussed before proceeding to the General Assembly. Should traditional elections be held, or should other methods be used? Should we just select from the list of 25 member of the Advocacy Committee? Who decides this when the new charter has not been approved by the General Assembly of the Federation? The government or the Church dignitaries? It was extremely difficult to impose this election on a church with a democratic tradition in the conference, most of which had passed the 42 great conferences in the Church's ninety-year history. Finally, the General Council would decide this.

- The next difficulty was the delegate issue. There were twenty-five years from the 42nd Conference to the 43rd Conference, with many changes in the organization of the Church. When it was independent, self-sustaining, or the beginning of the Church, setting up a list for the Church consisted of one or two delegates or no participants in the Council at that time. Of course, when it was heard there was a following Council a quarter of a century later, everyone wanted to attend. Therefore, the number of official delegates had to be stipulated to be reasonable. Moreover, according to the rules, the list of delegates had to be a priority to submit to the government before opening the conference, because this was the Administrative Council for elections, discussions, and votes related to the legislature of the Church. Not to mention the list of pastors and ministers was serving very well but was not accepted by the government. Resolving this was a difficult problem. No matter how difficult, though, it had to be at least temporarily resolved to conduct the General Council; the Council would resolve the rest of the problems. If not, they had to trust in God, for there is nothing that God cannot do.

After preparing everything, the historic day arrived that the children of God were waiting for: the first General Assembly of the General Federation (after 1975), or the forty-third according to Church history. The Great Council was held at Saigon Evangelical Church, 155 Tran Hung Dao, District 1, Ho Chi Minh City Lake Chi Minh, from 7–9 February 2001. The General Assembly opened in a solemn manner on the morning of February 8, 2001, at 8:00. The number of official delegates, including pastors, preachers, and believers, were 481 people. In addition to the usual developments, this General Assembly focused on two important things, the approval of the new Charter and electing the Board Management of Federation churches.

Because there were a few times that too many things needed to be discussed with the new charter, even with enthusiasm, the original rules were passed on regarding the charter, rules, religious law, and discipline, saving time to conduct the election. The second part was quite tough for the council: how to elect members? That was to vote for each position, by vote closed both round of nomination and election, not just present few then elect. This required much time.

The second way was to choose twenty-three pastors within the twenty-five members of the Advocacy Committee. It would be faster, and the government would approve it more easily. Finally, the General Council adopted the first means of holding an election after Pastor Nguyen Xuan Vong asked the General Assembly's decision on behalf of the Advocacy Committee.

Indeed, this was the historic council, ruled by God in each moment. The election lasted until about 22:00. Through the closing hours, the election was still incomplete according to the timeline; 19:00 was the beginning of the closing conference. Therefore, when it was time to vote the second round to choose the members that were more than half, the Council approved doubling the number of votes, so the rest would be more than half, as prescribed. If it had to proceed another round, the conference would last until midnight.

The election results for the new board management period (2001–2005 period) were as follows:

Head Leader: Pastor Pham Xuan Thieu

Vice Leader I: Pastor Duong Thanh

Vice Leader II: Pastor Tang Van Hi

General Secretary: Pastor Thai Phuoc Truong

Deputy Secretary General: Pastor Le Van Thien

General Treasurer: Pastor Phan Quang Thieu

Deputy General Treasurer: Pastor Le Cao Quy

Commissioners

Pastor Ksor Brao Pastor Nguyen Lam Huong

Pastor Le Khac Cung Preacher Tang Nguyen Tien

Pastor Ma Phuc Tin Pastor Ngo Van Buu

Pastor Ha Brong Pastor Tran Ba Thanh

Pastor Lê Hoàng Long Pastor Lưu Văn Ciáo

Pastor Le Khac Hoa Pastor Nguyen Van Dai

Pastor Nguyen Huu Vien Pastor Nguyen Ngoc Thuan

Pastor Nguyen Van Thanh Van Preacher Tran Nghia

After the election was completed, the delegates took a short break in place to continue entering the closing program. The closing program of the General Council played out well, although it went late. In addition to worship items, followed by the confession of the Head Leader Pastor Pham Xuan Thieu, the General Council attended the Eucharist before the ending. The Great Council closed with joy and gratitude to God. This was indeed a historic council; God had covered on the Council in every period. Nobody thought it could end quite so well.

Thus, the steps towards the Church have been completed. The charter was approved by the General Council, and the Board Management of the Federation was voted in. To be recognized as a person/legal entity, both items above had to be approved by the government.

IV. Legal Status

After more than a month of waiting, on March 16, 2001, the Vietnamese Evangelical Church (South) was officially recognized with legal status by the State of The Socialist Republic of Vietnam, according to Decision No. 15-QD / TGCP. Following the spirit of the decision, the government recognized the Charter and the General Management of the Federation were elected.

Following the good news about legal recognition documents, the Board Management of the General Federation prepared to hold a Welcome Ceremony to receive legal status and celebrate Ninety Years of Gospel Transmission to Vietnam. The ceremony was organized solemnly in the morning and afternoon of April 3, 2001.

From here, the Church entered a new stage with both advantages and challenges. Many people thought that, if we had legal status, we could do anything, but actually, the Vietnamese Evangelical Church (South) had to act within the legal framework of the Socialist Republic of Vietnam (Article 1 of the recognition legal status). Therefore, the Church had to continue to pray about the encouragement and development of the Church in this new period. At all levels, even the government had to have the correct opinion about the church. They could not keep looking at the church in prejudice as before.

BAN TÔN GIÁO CỦA CHÍNH PHỦ

DANH SÁCH THÀNH VIÊN

BAN TRỊ SỰ TỔNG LIÊN HỘI HỘI THÁNH TIN LÀNH VIỆT NAM (MIỀN NAM)

(Đính kèm theo Quyết định số 15 QĐ/TGCP ngày 16/3/2001 của Trưởng Ban Tôn giáo của Chính phủ)

Số tt	Họ và tên	Năm sinh	Chỗ ở hiện nay	Chức vụ	Chức danh BTS Tổng Liên hội
1.	Phạm Xuân Thiều	1944	112 Hoàng Diệu, Quận 4, TP HCM	Mục sư	Hội trưởng
2.	Dương Thạnh	1933	184 Ông Ích Khiêm, Đà Nẵng	Mục sư	Phó Hội trưởng thứ nhất
3	Tăng Văn Hy	1942	35 Nguyễn Đình Chiểu, TX Bến Tre	Mục sư	Phó Hội trưởng thứ hai
4.	Thái Phước Trường	1953	716A Hậu Giang, Q6, TP HCM	Mục sư	Tổng Thư ký
5.	Lê Văn Thiện	1951	325 Lê Thánh Phương, Nha Trang	Mục sư	Phó Tổng Thư ký
6.	Phan Quang Thiệu	1947	155 Trần Hưng Đạo, Q1, TP HCM	Mục sư	Tổng Thủ quỹ
7.	Lê Cao Quý	1941	56 Điện Biên Phủ, Đà Nẵng	Mục sư	Phó Tổng Thủ quỹ
8.	K'Sor Brao	1940	Trần Quốc Toản, Phú Bổn, Gia Lai	Mục sư	Ủy viên
9.	Nguyễn Lâm Hương	1945	2 Hùng Vương, TX Long Xuyên	Mục sư	Ủy viên
10.	Lê Khắc Cung	1926	Thôn 9, xã Hoà Phú, Chư Gút, Đắk Lắk	Mục sư	Ủy viên
11.	Nguyễn Tăng Tiến	1951	97 Ngô Quyền., Q5, TP Hồ Chí Minh	Truyền đạo	Ủy viên
12.	Mã Phúc Tín	1939	708 Phan Chu Trinh, Tam Kỳ	Mục sư	Ủy viên
13.	Ngô Văn Bửu	1940	236 Nguyễn Huệ, P2, TX Cao Lãnh	Mục sư	Ủy viên
14.	Ha Brong	1922	2/4 Thôn 4,Nơ Thôn Ha,Đức Trọng, Lâm Đồng	Mục sư	Ủy viên
15.	Trần Bá Thành	1935	635, đường 3/2, Q 10, TP Hồ Chí Minh	Mục sư	Ủy viên
16.	Lê Hoàng Long	1943	87 Xô Viết Nghệ Tĩnh, Cần Thơ	Mục sư	Ủy viên
17.	Lưu Văn Giáo	1943	30 Lê Thánh Phương, Nha Trang	Mục sư	Ủy viên
18.	Lê Khắc Hoá	1940	Tân Thiện, Hàm Tân, Bình Thuận	Mục sư	Ủy viên
19.	Nguyễn Văn Hai	1954	117/2 đường 1, Tân Bình, TP Hồ Chí Minh	Mục sư	Ủy viên
20.	Nguyễn Hữu Viễn	1942	102 Trần Phú, Long Khánh, Đồng Nai	Mục sư	Ủy viên
21.	Nguyễn Ngọc Thuận	1946	Trung Ái, Nhơn Hoà, An Nhơn, Bình Định	Mục sư	Ủy viên
22.	Nguyễn Văn Thanh Vân	1939	18B/3 khu 7, TT Cai Lậy, Tiền Giang	Mục sư	Ủy viên
23.	Trần Nghĩa	1950	34 Lạc Long Quân, Tân Bình, TP HCM	Truyền đạo	Ủy viên

Tổng số 23 người

BAN TÔN GIÁO CỦA CHÍNH PHỦ
ꕥ✱ꕥ
Số : 15 QĐ/TGCP

CỘNG HOÀ XÃ HỘI CHỦ NGHĨA VIỆT NAM
Độc lập - Tự do - Hạnh phúc
-------★★★------

Hà Nội, ngày 16 tháng 3 năm 2001

QUYẾT ĐỊNH

Về việc công nhận tư cách pháp nhân của Hội thánh Tin lành Việt Nam (miền Nam)

TRƯỞNG BAN TÔN GIÁO CỦA CHÍNH PHỦ

- Căn cứ Nghị định số 26/1999/NĐ-CP ngày 19 tháng 4 năm 1999 của Chính phủ về các hoạt động tôn giáo;

- Thừa uỷ quyền của Thủ tướng Chính phủ tại công văn số 05/CP-NC ngày 19 tháng 1 năm 2001;

- Xét đề nghị của Hội thánh Tin lành Việt Nam (miền Nam) tại văn thư đề ngày 12 tháng 02 năm 2001.

QUYẾT ĐỊNH

Điều 1: Chấp thuận Hội thánh Tin lành Việt Nam (miền Nam) hoạt động trong khuôn khổ luật pháp của Nước Cộng hoà xã hội chủ nghĩa Việt Nam, theo Hiến chương được thông qua tại Đại hội đồng lần thứ I/2001 (lần thứ 43 theo lịch sử Giáo hội) và đã được phê chuẩn (toàn văn Hiến chương kèm theo).

Điều 2: Chấp thuận nhân sự Ban Trị sự Tổng Liên hội Hội thánh Tin lành Việt Nam (miền Nam) gồm 23 (hai mươi ba) người được bầu cử tại Đại hội đồng Tổng Liên hội Hội thánh Tin lành Việt Nam (miền Nam) lần thứ I/2001 (lần thứ 43 theo lịch sử Giáo hội), có danh sách kèm theo.

Điều 3: Chủ tịch Uỷ ban Nhân dân các tỉnh, thành phố trực thuộc Trung ương - nơi có tín đồ, mục sư, truyền đạo Hội thánh Tin lành Việt Nam (miền Nam) và Ban Trị sự Tổng Liên hội Hội thánh Tin lành Việt Nam (miền Nam) chịu trách nhiệm thi hành quyết định này.

Điều 4: Quyết định này có hiệu lực kể từ ngày ký ./.

Nơi nhận:
- Tổng Liên hội Hội thánh Tin lành Việt Nam (miền Nam);
- Như Điều 3;
- Lưu VT, VTL.

TRƯỞNG BAN

Lê Quang Vịnh

Chứng thực bản sao đúng với bản chính.
Số chứng thực...498...Quyển số 04 SCT/BS
Ngày...4...tháng...01...năm...2007
KT.CHỦ TỊCH UBND P.12 - Q.4
PHÓ CHỦ TỊCH

Nguyễn Hoàng Xuân Vinh

Hội thánh Tin Lành Việt Nam (miền Nam) nhận tư cách pháp nhân

Ảnh VIỆT DŨNG

The General Management of the Federation had to face many issues, including backlogs of the past few decades. Current affairs must be resolved; many plans for the future of God's children were stuck for decades. The future orientation of the General Management of Federation churches in the four-year term was as follows:

1. Establishment of Representative Board and Human Resources present for provinces and cities.

2. Recovering the churches that have not been able to operate normally.

3. Constructing churches and chapels for the places crowded by believers and far from the main church.

4. Ordering the opening of a Biblical Theological Seminary and Bible classes in local areas to train God's servants.

5. Ordaining pastors and solve the problem of presiding for the churches without official leaders.

6. Ordering the aging pastors and equipping new pastors to serve.

7. Publishing Christian literature.

8. The problem of accommodation for the retired pastors and pastors' widows and preachers.

9. Research and promote the direction to develop the Church.

10. Actively contribute to improve the Church's social life.

One note was that, although the Vietnam Evangelical Church had legal status, many churches belonging to the Vietnamese Evangelical Church were still not accepted by the government, especially the churches on the Highland. They had to ask and wait for the government. Considering and accepting each church one by one, was a prolonged process that has continued until now. Of course, this is different from the case of opening a new church later when the Southern Vietnamese Evangelical Church had legal status.

In fact, despite the Vietnamese Evangelical Church (South) having a charter, rules, and discipline, compared to the old charter, it was too new in processing, so for the Board Management of the General Federation, it was also quite hard to stabilize the local church in the new period to follow the new Charter. In terms of the government, not a few local officers performed state policy for the Church from the central government to the local, from government decrees on religious affairs to the Charter of the Vietnamese Evangelical Church approved by the government. Because of the newness inside and outside, the new Board Management of the Federation churches was wholeheartedly relying on God, trying every means to stabilize and develop the Church in a new phase with many challenges.

V. Ordaining a New Pastor

Since 1975, the ordination of a pastor met many difficulties, although the graduation program of the General Federation was issued for uneducated preachers. The Church's need for ministry was huge, because it related to marriages, baptisms, and blessings that preachers could not perform. Moreover, since 2001, there was no Preacher title, only three titles: Pastor, New Pastor, and Female Preacher.

Therefore, a very important decision of the Board Management at that time was "recognizing 158 pastors" (New Pastor), specifically for a New Pastor to perform three sacraments and ceremonies exclusively for pastors at his church, to resolve the deadlock while waiting for the ordination of Pastors in the coming days (Protocol 3/2001 / BB_BTSTLH meeting from April 4, 2001). However, when enforcing the protocol, the Board Management faced many difficulties on the governmental side, because the government said that the recognition of 158 pastor was a legal violation. They thought that was the same as ordinating a true pastor without submitting documents to the government. However, this was only a change of the title of a minister or preacher to a new pastor. It was not a ceremony, because in the Charter, there was no Preacher title. The Board Management of the General Federation had to explain the issue many times, and it took a long time for the Religion Committee of the provinces and cities to understand and sympathize, especially after many true Pastor ordinations.

VI. The Death of Pastor Pham Xuan Thieu

Since taking office as head leader of the Vietnamese Evangelical Church (South), Head Leader Pastor Pham Xuan Thieu and standing and the permanent members of the Federation faced too much stress and pressure from outside and inside the Church. Anonymous letters were harming the work of God in general and pastors in particular. From the 43rd Conference of the General Council, while the general Church rejoiced in the good results that God gave them, there were a few who resisted by sending many anonymous letters to smear and slander the members of the General Federation, especially the key people, to reduce the spirit of the Lord's servants. Even these people claimed that the General Council was not in God's will. Despite knowing that anonymous mail was not worth the worry, the devil wanted to harm God's people and His work. Someone even opened a website with spiritual names, but the content was no encouragement.

A paramount accident of the Evangelical Church of Vietnam was the loss of head leader Pastor Pham Xuan Thieu (in June 2002) after four months in the office. This was a huge loss for the Church when it had just entered a period in which it needed to stabilize.

According to the provisions of the Charter, the General Management of the Federation had to re-elect one of the two vice leaders to become the head leader. At that time, the first vice leader was Pastor Duong Thanh, and the second was vice lead Pastor Tang Van Hi. After praying and voting by secret ballot, the result was that Pastor Duong Thanh was chosen by the Board Management to keep his position as the head leader of the Vietnamese Evangelical Church (South) after June 2002 to continue to lead the Church in the next phase.

VII. Difficulties

Some pastors went to the Kingdom of God, like Pastor Pham Xuan Thieu, President; Pastor Le Khac Cung; Pastor Ha Brong; and Pastor Ksor Brao, Commissioner, the General Management of the Federation still thanked God for continuing to guide the General Federation to stabilize and develop the Church. During the quarter of a century, there was a General Council, so everything was remade from the beginning, and there was too much work to be done. Therefore, the Board Management of the General Federation had to choose the priority work to do.

- One of the priorities was to nominate a Representative Committee and Personnel Presentative Committee of 32 provinces (nowadays 34) because in the new Charter, there was no longer a county mechanism. When there was county before, most jobs were chosen before submitting them to the General Federation. Consequently, the role of the current representatives' committee was needed to share the burden of the work with the General Federation in development. Compared to the church before 1975, the number of Christians and Churches had greatly increased, from 146,089 to about 1,000,000, although it was just an "extended arm" of the General Federation. However, there was no administrative authority like the previous County.

The new charter stipulates five pastors, and seven pastors in the Permanent General Federation must work full time for the position in the Federation. With 16 commissioners, there was too much work for a growing church in a rather difficult period. Therefore, the General Management of the Federation had to resolve problems in the long run since 1975, as well as finding directions to build and develop the Church in the new period, with opportunities and risks confused both spiritually and organizationally, especially in the new millennium, with its many challenges.

The Number of Christians From 1910-2010

Although the Evangelical Church of Vietnam (South) already had legal status, the Church in the Highland in general and Dak-lak in particular was experiencing difficulties.

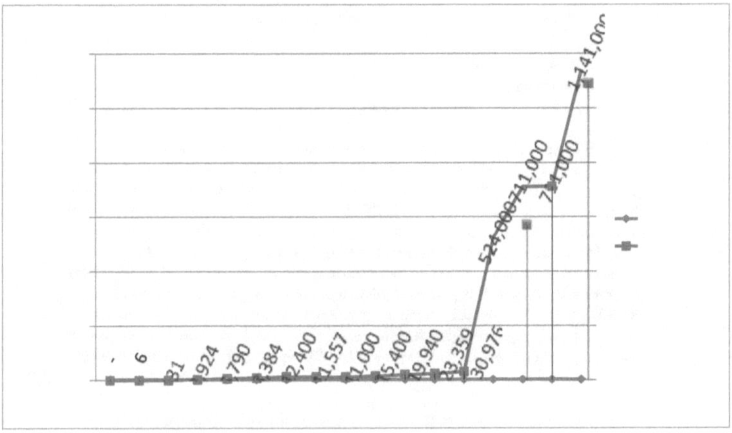

HỘI THÁNH TIN LÀNH VIỆT NAM (MIỀN NAM)
TỔNG LIÊN HỘI

Số: 747/2002/TLH-TT.

CỘNG HÒA XÃ HỘI CHỦ NGHĨA VIỆT NAM
Độc lập – Tự do – Hạnh phúc

TP. Hồ Chí Minh, ngày 19 tháng 10 năm 2002

<u>*Kính gửi:*</u> - THỦ TƯỚNG CHÍNH PHỦ
- BAN TÔN GIÁO CỦA CHÍNH PHỦ

<u>*Đồng kính gửi:*</u> - ỦY BAN NHÂN DÂN tỉnh ĐĂK LĂK
- BAN TÔN GIÁO & DÂN TỘC ĐĂK LĂK

THƯ KIẾN NGHỊ

V/V. CÁC HỘI THÁNH TIN LÀNH TẠI ĐĂK LĂK BỊ NGĂN CẤM SINH HOẠT TÔN GIÁO.

Thưa Thủ tướng và quí cấp Chính quyền,

Thay cho toàn thể giáo dân thuộc Hội thánh Tin lành Việt Nam (miền Nam), chúng tôi chân thành cám ơn quí cấp Chính quyền đã giúp đỡ giáo hội chúng tôi suốt 27 năm qua.

Nay, chúng tôi kính xin Thủ tướng và Quí vị vui lòng kiên nhẫn xem xét toàn bộ phần giải trình như sau:

Gần đây, các Hội thánh Tin lành tại ĐăkLăk đã gặp rất nhiều khó khăn, từ cá nhân giáo dân đến các nhà nguyện vốn sinh hoạt bình thường *hơn 20 năm qua*, nay hầu hết đều bị cấm đoán. Khi trước, tuy có sự ngăn trở nhưng họ vẫn được nhóm lại, dầu là vào ngày thường trong tuần. Tính đến 1/10/2001, toàn tỉnh có trên 135.792 giáo dân và hơn 412 Chi hội, nay chỉ còn 58 nơi tạm sinh hoạt, 354 Chi hội đã bị đóng cửa (tỷ lệ: 6/7) và số này tiếp tục gia tăng. Các địa phương đã tích cực nghiêm cấm không cho Hội thánh đặc biệt là người dân tộc, nhóm lại thờ phượng Đức Chúa Trời. Ban Đại diện Tin lành (được công nhận) đã trình lên Chính quyền tỉnh và Chính phủ, nhưng rồi sự bất bớ vẫn tiếp diễn ngày càng nhiều hơn: các nhà nguyện bị đóng cửa, các quản nhiệm bị giam giữ và khủng bố về tinh thần lẫn vật chất, giáo dân không được gặp mặt và liên hệ với nhau, tiền phạt gia tăng do tiếp tục nhóm lại thờ phượng Chúa. Có nơi buộc giáo dân phải bỏ đạo bằng nhiều hình thức: uống máu dê tế thần, lạm dụng mô hình *Làng văn hóa - không tôn giáo*, cấm cản đi lễ hàng tuần, tịch thu kinh sách, dùng các phương tiện thông tin đại chúng trong Tỉnh như báo đài để bôi nhọ, kích động quần chúng chống lại Tin lành. ..

Thưa Quí vị, giáo hội chúng tôi thật đau lòng khi thấy sự ngăn cấm sinh hoạt bình thường của đạo Tin lành cứ tiếp diễn ngày càng qui mô. Giáo dân vốn phấn khởi khi có tư cách pháp nhân, có Đại biểu chính thức tham dự các kỳ Đại Hội đồng, nay lại hoang mang, nghi ngại. Thể theo Hiến pháp và Chính sách *tôn trọng tự do tín ngưỡng, tôn giáo*, chúng tôi đã phản ánh với Ban Tôn giáo Trung ương và mòn mỏi chờ đợi Chính phủ can thiệp.

Chúng tôi tự hỏi, Giáo dân tại vùng cao đã phạm tội gì để bị đối xử như vậy? - Phải chăng do theo Đêga? Xin thưa: Ngay từ đầu, Giáo hội đã khẳng định về Đêga qua thông báo số 7/01/TLH-BTS ngày 5/4/2001 và tất cả Giáo dân đều thuận phục. - Hoặc do tiếp tục sinh hoạt tôn giáo mà chưa có phép? Xin thưa: Hơn 20 năm qua, họ đã nhóm lại đều đặn như vậy, chỉ với một mục đích là thờ phượng Đức Chúa Trời dựa trên Kinh Thánh mà Nhà nước đã cho phép in và phổ biến. Nhiều lần nhất là sau Đại Hội đồng 2001, chúng tôi cũng đã trình danh sách giáo dân và nhà nguyện lên quí cấp Chính quyền mà nhu cầu chính đáng của giáo dân vẫn chưa được cứu xét và đáp ứng.

1/

- Phải chăng giáo dân Tin lành đặc biệt người sắc tộc là kẻ thù nguy hiểm của xã hội? Xin khẳng định: mỗi giáo dân đều là công dân tốt, đáng tin cậy vì được Kinh Thánh răn dạy: "*Mọi người phải vâng phục nhà cầm quyền, vì tin rằng mọi quyền đều do Đức Chúa Trời chỉ định và các quan quyền là chức việc của Đức Chúa Trời, để làm ích cho người*" (*Rôma 13.1,4 - tóm tắt*). Tin lành thực sự đổi mới tấm lòng của kẻ tin. Họ từ bỏ các hủ tục, mê tín dị đoan, các thói hư tật xấu để sống cuộc đời lành mạnh, trong sáng. Tin lành của Đức Chúa Trời ban sự bình an, thánh hóa và chữa lành về tâm linh lẫn thể xác cho mọi người. Có thể nói như tên gọi, Tin lành có tính cách mạng triệt để tốt lành, vì đặt căn bản trên *tình yêu và sự chết chuộc tội cho mọi người, cùng sự sống lại của Chúa Cứu thế Giê-xu*. Đây là nội dung niềm tin, sự sống đạo và truyền đạo của mỗi giáo dân. Họ chân thật, hiền hoà nhưng dứt khoát khước từ những gì trái với niềm tin hay liên quan đến sự cúng tế, thờ hình tượng; nếu có kết tội họ, thì chỉ có thể buộc tội trong lãnh vực này mà thôi.

Thưa Thủ tướng và quí cấp Chính quyền,

Tin lành đã có tại Việt Nam hơn 91 năm qua. Thiết tưởng, sự kiện ĐakLăk hôm nay có thể tác động không chỉ trong nước mà còn lây lan cả ngoài nước và khắp thế giới. Vì vậy,

- Căn cứ Hiến pháp nước Cộng hoà xã hội chủ nghĩa Việt Nam, điều 70, ngày 15/4/1992: "*Công dân có quyền tự do tín ngưỡng, tôn giáo, theo hoặc không theo một tôn giáo nào. Các tôn giáo đều bình đẳng trước pháp luật. Những nơi thờ tự của các tín ngưỡng, tôn giáo được pháp luật bảo hộ. Không ai được xâm phạm tự do tín ngưỡng, tôn giáo hoặc lợi dụng tín ngưỡng, tôn giáo để làm trái pháp luật và chính sách của Nhà nước*";
- Căn cứ chính sách trước sau như một: "*tự do tín ngưỡng, tôn giáo và công bằng xã hội*";
- Căn cứ công văn số 398/CV-TGCP, điều 7c, ngày 16/7/2001 của Ban Tôn giáo Chính phủ: "*Ở các tỉnh Tây nguyên . . . Những nơi mới theo đạo trong thời gian gần đây thì **giữ nguyên trạng** ...*" (chứ không phải xóa bỏ);

Chúng tôi khẩn thiết xin Chính phủ can thiệp để các sinh hoạt giáo hội Tin lành tại ĐakLăk sớm được bình thường, các nhà thờ được xây dựng để đáp ứng nhu cầu bức xúc của giáo dân.

Chân thành cám ơn và rất mong sớm nhận được sự trả lời của quí vị. Trân trọng kính chào.

TM BAN TRỊ SỰ TỔNG LIÊN HỘI
QUYỀN HỘI TRƯỞNG,

Mục sư Dương Thanh

2

HỘI THÁNH TIN LÀNH VIỆT NAM (MIỀN NAM)
TỔNG LIÊN HỘI
155 Trần Hưng Đạo, Quận 1, TP. Hồ Chí Minh
Tel: 08-8369585; 8365178 - Fax: 08-8373180
E-mail: vptlh@hcm.fpt.vn

Số: 752/2002/TLH-TT
V/v.-Xin cầu nguyện đặc biệt cho Viện Thần học & các HT tại Đăk Lăk.

CỘNG HÒA XÃ HỘI CHỦ NGHĨA VIỆT NAM
Độc lập – Tự do – Hạnh phúc

Tp. Hồ Chí Minh, ngày 23 tháng 10 năm 2002

Kính gửi:

Quản nhiệm, Ban Trị sự - Chấp sự &
Quí Tín hữu tại Hội thánh Tin Lành

Thưa quí Hội thánh,

Một trong những điều mà Hội thánh chúng ta hằng quan tâm là việc mở lại Thần học viện. Ban Trị sự Tổng Liên hội đã cầu nguyện và nỗ lực chuẩn bị cho việc này, cũng như liên hệ với các cấp Chính quyền. Mọi thủ tục về hành chánh đã xong và Ban Tôn giáo của Chính phủ đã hứa sẽ có giấy phép trong Quí 4 này.

Tiếp theo, chúng tôi được biết thời gian gần đây, các Chi hội tại *Đăk Lăk* đã gặp rất nhiều khó khăn. Tính đến 1/10/2001, toàn tỉnh có trên 135.792 tín hữu với hơn 412 Chi hội thì nay chỉ còn 56 nơi tạm sinh hoạt, số còn lại phải giải tán để thờ phượng tại nhà và số này tiếp tục gia tăng. Các tín hữu - đặc biệt là người dân tộc tại đây, không được nhóm lại thờ phượng Chúa. Ban Đại diện Tin Lành đã trình lên Chính phủ nhưng sự bắt bớ càng thêm: các nhà nguyện bị đóng cửa, các quản nhiệm bị khủng bố về tinh thần lẫn vật chất, một số bị giam giữ, các tín hữu không được nhóm lại, nếu vẫn nhóm thì chịu phạt nặng..

Chúng ta thật đau lòng khi thấy sinh hoạt của các Chi hội tại ĐăkLăk bị ngăn cấm. Thường Trực Tổng Liên hội đã gởi Thư Kiến nghị trình Thủ Tướng, Ban Tôn giáo của Chính Phủ và Chính quyền tỉnh ĐăkLăk. Nay, chúng tôi nài xin toàn thể Hội thánh dành nhiều thì giờ ***cầu nguyện đặc biệt*** cho hai vấn đề nêu trên như II Sử 7.14 đã chép: ***"Nhược bằng dân sự Ta là dân gọi bằng danh Ta, hạ mình xuống, cầu nguyện, tìm kiếm mặt Ta và trở lại, bỏ con đường tà thì Ta ở trên trời sẽ nghe, tha thứ tội chúng nó và cứu xứ họ khỏi tai vạ".*** Sức mạnh của chúng ta ở tại sự cầu nguyện, một lòng một ý và tại nếp sống Đạo tinh sạch, thuần nhất. Chúng ta tin rằng Đức Chúa Trời Toàn Năng sẽ nhậm lời nài xin của Hội thánh.

Xin chân thành cám ơn và trân trọng kính chào Quí vị.

TM. BAN TRỊ SỰ TỔNG LIÊN HỘI
TỔNG THƯ KÝ,

Mục sư Thái Phước Trường

According to a report from the Representative Committee about the actual situation in this province, this was one of largest number of Christians of the Evangelical Church of Vietnam South, about 150,000 people, so there were many difficulties when worshiping God. The government ordered to close most places, consisting of 412 churches and small worship groups. If they continued to worship, they would be recorded, fined, or punished with other measures.

The church in Daklak and all churches prayed for this. Finally, the General Federation sent a document to the Central Government and all levels in the province to resolve the tension and unusual problems in the province at that time. Frequently, the Board Management would work with many government levels, and the Lord's work in Dak-Lak province was solved step by step.

The Protest at Dak-lak in 2014

Since the Vietnamese Evangelical Church (MN) qualified for legal status, the common activities of the Church were more stable on some sides. However, God's work in the Highland provinces still met certain difficulties compared with the Kinh Church, although the Kinh Church or the church of ethnic groups was still "one" with the organization of the Vietnamese Evangelical Church, having the same

Charter. Thanks to God, the Church in the Highland provinces has still grown very strong among its many difficulties.

After a short time, in April 2010, the situation of the Church in Dak-Lak was unstable when protests occurred in Buon Me Thuot. Of course, it was not quite the religion problem, as not just Protestant Christians joined this protest. Ethnic Christians also participated in the protest. Apart from the reasons of land and other issues, it perhaps was also because of the difficulties and limits in worshiping God. First, some people in the government suspected that this was the plan of the Federation Church. Then, permanent members of the General Federation came to Buon Me Thuot to work with the government to prove that the stance of the Church was a political and the government should create better conditions for these God's children in the activity of worshiping God, to improve the situation of the churches in Dak Lak.

In general, there were many reasons why God's work in the Highland provinces struggled after 1975, even after the legalizing of the Church. But there was one thing that we could not deny, no matter whose view it was: The Lord's Church has still grown among its difficulties. Thank God for His grace and help that the Church could overcome everything and still develop. In addition to the grace, help, preservation of God, and the faith in God of the

Christians, we recognize the objective comment of the authors in the *Past to present* magazine, number 370, December 2010. The very interesting question was "Why do so many ethnic minorities in the Highlands follow the Evangelism (maybe understood as the "CM&A Protestant Gospel" in this sentence) and develop so fast?"

The following numbers show not only the difference but also a significant increase in the number of Protestant believers in ethnic minorities in the Highlands in recent years. In 2004, 15 percent of the province's population was Christian ("Christian" might be understood both as Roman Catholic Roman and Protestant), of which ethnic minorities made up 14.3 percent. In 2009, the corresponding rate was 15.9 percent for the local population and 16.2 percent for ethnic minorities. Meanwhile, in 2004, the number of Protestants in the Highlands was only 6.5 percent of the population, which increased to 7.2 percent of the population. It is worth mentioning that the growth was just concentrated only in ethnic minorities. In 2004, Protestant faiths encompassed ethnic minorities, accounting for 9.3 percent of the population of this religion. By 2009, this rate had increased to 21.1 percent.

Also, notably, if Christians were ethnic minorities accounting for only 31 percent, while the rate of Protestantism was 89.4 percent, many localities and Protestant believers were ethnic minorities in very high rates, as follows: Gia Lai at 98.3 percent and Dak-Lak at 90.5 percent. Thus, in 2009, regarding the total of 362,689 people who were Protestants in the Highlands, most of them were ethnic minorities, 6.5 times more than Protestants throughout the territory of Vietnam in 1954. Currently, nearly one-fourth of the population of eleven ethnic minorities in the Highlands are Protestant.

One question of great concern is why ethnic minorities followed Protestantism in the Highlands so quickly. We can easily find the answer in documents about taking advantage of political forces during a time of war. But this explanation is still relevant when the Gospel in the Highlands developed faster when the country was peaceful and just in a period of the new transformation, industrialization, and modernization. The social phenomenon was always rooted in the communing itself. Whether from a religious or cultural perspective, objectively, it was undeniable that this religion responded to the cultural and spiritual life of ethnic minorities in the Highlands. Or more accurately, Protestants can only penetrate and develop in the ethnic minority community when they find the suitability in this religion that the teaching was in line with the traditional concepts that have been deeply ingrained in them. If not, it is difficult for any type or general replacement "inherent mind" of native Highlanders who are honest, true, and gentle.

Perhaps we should say that there is no reason to discern education levels or other reasons to answer why many ethnic groups follow Protestantism. Because one thing seems paradoxical but very convenient: The lower the level of education, the more conservative people are. Holding on to old concepts, the past rituals are deeply ingrained in the blood. That has not been mentioned yet, that the current rate of educated people and educated ethnic minorities in the Highland is much higher than several decades ago. A point is also worth mentioning that Protestant followers in the Highlands are mainly young and middle-aged, next to the generation that continues, preserves, and promotes cultural heritage. Protestantism is a religion of love and compassion. Protestants are willing to share and support their friends through hardship and consider this a criterion of religious life. Protestantism promotes reason in faith. Salvation or problems come only by faith and prayer, not rules and rituals. Consequently, the way to practice the Gospel was quite simple, without any periodic, cumbersome things like other religions. This is also an advantage for the Gospel to easily be transmitted in the Highlands.

Therefore, we can see that, the people in the Highlands did not previously have a unique religion. Nonetheless, the appearance of the Gospel helped people find love for others, the spirit of charity, helping one’s community, and the recognition of God's power and miracles that solve the problems of life, all of which people generally need. These are the primary reasons they came to the Gospel, and the Gospel will continue to grow in the Highlands because Protestants believe that they have returned to the way that God originally intended. That is why we see Protestant missionaries and every Protestant believer is considered an active sower and focus as a missionary.

VIII. Re-Establishing the Theology Institute (Theological Seminary)

One of the things that the Board Management of the General Federations and the Church cared about was re-opening the theology institute, closed since 1976. The Board Management of General Federation nominated Pastor Thai Phuoc Truong as Secretary General and Pastor Le Cao Quy as Deputy Treasurer to contact the government to reopen the school. The two God's servants had to contact many concerned authorities many times to solve this problem. The problem is:

- The facilities of the Theological Seminary (Theology Institute) were currently governed by the State. The authorities wanted the Church to give this facility to the State.
- There would only be an open class, not a school (once, not continuous)

- We could not use the old name. The only name that could be used is the Bible School.
- The professor must have a degree, a function, and a pedagogy.
- Students must be accepted by the local government before considering Bible School.
- Locations had to respond to required standards.
- There must be regulations adopted by the government.
- Must be approved by the Ministry of Education and Training with university standards. There were many other issues that the government forced the church to respond to in reopening the Theological Seminary. But thank God, difficult problems were finally solved, when Pastor Thai Phuoc Truong and Pastor Le Cao Quy clearly and particularly explained each issue.
- In the immediate future, the need for training is more important than the facilities, so the work related to the Nha Trang Institute of Theology will be solved later, but no one dares to donate to the government, because this is a very sacred base of the church.
- The purpose and needs of the current church now had the legal status to open a regular training school for very large and long-term

needs like other religions. There was also legal status, not open classes once with the Church having to ask permission every time a class was started.

- The old name was "Theological Institute," and we could finally use the new name, "Biblical Theology Seminary."
- In terms of professors, there cannot be enough people who have a degree as required because for a long time after 1975, the Church was not allowed to send students overseas. Therefore, because this was the Theology Institute, the important requirement for professors was basic, profound, and theological depth rather than degrees but a lack of experience in the theological field of the Church. Referring to "academic rank," according to the Bible and organization, those nominated as professors were accepted by General Federation. In terms of "pedagogy," those who were appointed to be professors were also to be pastors with teaching processes and good communication ability.
- In terms of the students, there were still necessary requirements, as before. However, instead of being accepted first by the government, the General Federation required that the student must complete an examination and be approved by the church first, then submitted to the government to consider for citizenship.

After receiving the license, on February 14, 2003, the opening ceremony of the first school year (since 1975) organized solemnly at Saigon Evangelical Church. The number of students in the first course was 50, and the second course was allowed to enroll a hundred students. In the second course onwards, the government allowed 15 students of the Vietnamese Evangelical Church (North) to be sent to the Biblical and Theology Institute (South) for training. This is thanks to God, for the Vietnamese Evangelical Church (MB) could only open one class of Bible School from 1988 to 1993, terminated (with 15 people) until today.

Temporary Facility on the Fourth Floor of Sai Gon Church

The professors included Pastor Thai Phuoc Truong, Pastor Ngo Van Buu, Pastor Le Van Thien, Pastor Phan Quang Thieu, Pastor Le Cao Quy, Pastor Nguyen Ngoc Thuan, Pastor Tang Nguyen Tien, and Pastor Nguyen Lam Huong. The Assistant Committee included Pastor Dieu Huynh, Pastor Ha Kar, Pastor Ma Phuc Thanh Tuoi, New Pastor Le Tan, Pastor Trinh Chien, Pastor Phan Phung Hung, and Mrs. Kieu Thi Thai An. Teachers were Pastor Y Kyban, Pastor Tran Nghia, Doctor Le Hoang Son, and Mrs. Tran Thi Ly.

Thánh Kinh Thần Học Viện Nha Trang & Mô hình Viện Thánh Kinh Thần Học
Thực hiện: Sinh viên Khóa 1, Viện Thánh Kinh Thần Học, Hội Thánh Tin Lành Việt Nam (miền Nam)
Biên tập: Hồ Nguyên Kha; Võ Văn Kiếm Toàn; Nguyễn Duy Thiên Ân; Triệu Nguyên Thiên Phúc

The next concern was how to have a new facility worthy of a Theological Institute. In fact, getting back Nha Trang institute was not an easy and quick solution. Accordingly, the desire of the General Federation was to find a way to build a Theological Institute in Saigon first. The problems of land, finance, and licenses were too difficult. Consequently, it was more feasible to ask the government to return the Protestant Cemetery at Cat Lai (Binh Trung Ward, District 2, Ho Chi Minh City) to build a new Theological Institute. So, this plan lasted for many years, from the completion of procedures for land allocation, construction permit, finance encouragement, construction, etc. until March 2010, when the Theological Institute moved to a new place.

However, the Institute only completed a student dormitory, a school, and a library to temporarily operate while it continued to build one more block of residences and a church for the Institute in the future, as planned. The Protestant Cemetery's area is about 30,000 m2. The State only gave back a small part: 7,500 m, the current area of the Institute. This is a relatively small number compared to the need of the Institute, while the land area of the Nha Trang Seminary, which the State estimated to be requisitioning, is over 100,000 m2. However, this might still be acceptable for the initial re-establishment.

Another idea should be mentioned more: the transition of silently training to formal training. For a long time, since Nha Trang Institute and two Bible schools in Da Lat and Buon Me Thuot were closed, many of God's servants had to give up their work to make the training work silently. Therefore, when legal status was attained, the Institute was re-established, the General

Management of the Federation was submitted, and the government allowed the theological supplement for those who received training during this time. Therefore, the Theological Institute opened eight Theological Supplementary Centers in Da Nang, Gia Lai, Dak-läk, Dak-Nong, Lam Dong, Binh Phuoc, Khanh Hoa, and TP. Ho Chi Minh. After two years, many theological complementary courses were completed, in full compliance of the regulations. Volunteer preachers were graduated, and the General Federation recognized titles and assignments as well as public administration received for official services in the churches. This number has significantly met the need for the Lord's servants during this critical period, alongside formal graduates of graduation courses after 2006.

The Relationship with the Foreign Church

It can be said that, after 1975, the Vietnamese Evangelical Church's relationship with overseas communities was very limited. The Church stood entirely on its own feet to build and develop itself. Since 1927, the Church has been independent and separate from the Federation of the Evangelical Union or administrative organizations. However, the Federation of the Evangelical Church Union still stood by to provide financial support as well as other areas until 1975 when it ended. Not only the Evangelical Union, but all the other Christian organizations that have ever cooperated with the Church before, were no longer connected. Until

Vietnam was renewed, especially since the Church obtained legal status, the relationship of the Vietnamese Evangelical Church with foreign churches and other Christian organizations has been incrementally improved.

IX. The 44th General Conference of the General Assembly

After four years of the first term, 2001–2005, the General Management of the Federation tried to implement the orientations set out, but there were still many things to continue to be done in the next term. The 44th General Conference of the General Federation (the second since 1975) was organized solemnly at the Saigon Evangelical Church; it was held from March 1–4, 2005. There were 821 formal delegates, and about 500 informal delegates from 34 provinces of the South were pleased to attend the conference. The theme was "Looking at Jesus Christ."

The speaker of the General Conference was Head Leader Pastor Duong Thanh and General Secretary Le Van Thien. The results of the Board Management of the General Federation for the term 2005– 2009 are as follows:

President Pastor Thai Phuoc Truong

Vive President I Pastor Ngo Van Buu

Vice President II Pastor Tang Van Hi

Secretary General Pastor Le Van Thien

Deputy Secretary General Pastor Le Cao Quy

General Treasurer Pastor Phan Quang Thieu

Deputy General Treasurer Pastor Phan Vinh Cu

Commissioners

Preacher Tang Nguyen Tien Pastor Nguyen Ngoc Thuan

Pastor Tran Nghia Pastor Ma Phuc Tin

Pastor Le Hoang Long Pastor Nguyen Huu Vien

Pastor Siu Y Kim Pastor Dieu Huynh

Pastor Luu Tu An Pastor Y Ky Êban

Pastor Le Khac Hoa Pastor Nguyen Van Thanh Van

Pastor Nguyen Van Ngoc Pastor Nguyen Xuan Sanh

Pastor R. Mah Loan.

The General Council has spent much time discussing the changing plan or future plans, which were kept or continued, one of the issues that the General Council cared about was that the churches and facilities of the Church were requisitioned by the State, especially the Biblical Theology Seminary of Nha Trang and the No. 7 Church on Tran Cao Van Street. Then the Council voted: to "concurrently request the government of the Socialist Republic of Vietnam to give back to the Evangelical Church 217 facilities that have been taken over, including the Biblical Theology Seminary."

In addition, there were many ideas of this General Council related to the work of managing God's work, including "increasing the members of the Permanent staff from 5 people to 7 people and asking the Permanent staff to serve full-time." The Board Management of the General Federation was entrusted to adjust the internal rules and regulations to vote for the Representative Board of the provinces and cities. The General Council also entrusted the General Federation to search for the construction and relocation of the Headquarters of the Federation to a new location.

Especially in this conference, there were many of the Lord's servants from foreign countries who attended and spoke: Head Leader of the CM&A in the USA Peter Norris Nanfelt, Pastor Thomas Stebbin, and Pastor Nguyen Anh Tai, head leader of the American County Church.

Thereafter, the Board Management sent requests to the Prime Minister and all levels of government to give back 265 churches and facilities in the last General Council, such as:

- Churches and facilities that were still intact but not made available.
- Places that were misused as Tradition Centers and cooperatives.
- Places that were leveled, with facilities built on the Church's land.

However, after many years and many requests submitted to various government levels, the General Federation has not yet been answered rightly or satisfactorily. Actually, the government has returned a very few facilities of the original 265. Priority locations were still not returned, like the Biblical Theology Seminary of Nha Trang and No. 7 church on Tran Cao Van. Moreover, while the Church was asking and waiting for the government to return the churches and facilities above, some local governments were ordered to destroy the churches and the facilities, which were still intact, such as the Missionary Center of the Cham people in Phuoc Dong (Ninh Thuan), Ben Cat Evangelical Church (Binh Duong), Thap Cham Evangelical Church (Ninh Thuan), Dong Tam Evangelical Church (Ho Chi Minh City), the Bible School in Da Lat (Lam Dong), and the only church of the Ede Christians in Buon Me Thuot.

Ben Cat Church – Binh Duong

Orphanage Church (Left) and Thap Cham Church (right)

Moreover, in this period, the Ordinance on Belief and Religion was issued (2005) according to Decree 22 of the government. This was a new turning point for the legal framework of the State on religion. However, the local government did not yet work synchronously. The "please" did not apply exactly the new Ordinance and Decree.

In this period, the churches were opening many "Team Points." Thanks to that, in the following years, Group Points were eligible to become "Branches" and continue to add to the "Association" in the organization of the Association Vietnamese Protestant Saints (MN). Therefore, the general assembly approved to move forward with such strategy.

X. Establishing the *Pastoral News*

For a long time, the news of the church was widely popularized. By the end of 2004, the Evangelical Church of Vietnam (South) was licensed to publish the *Pastoral News* monthly with content like spiritual devotions and news of the Church all around the world to praise and pray. Although it was not a newspaper with a large distribution, it provided information about the current situation of the Church.

Ministry 2005 Magazine

XI. Evangelizing Outside the Church

There was an optimistic breakthrough for the church for a long time from 1975 until now. The Church was allowed to preach the Gospel in public places like the missionary campaigns of old. Based on the legal framework for public preaching, the Church did pray and request permission from the government in Ho Chi Minh City to organize an evangelistic event for Christmas. By 2005, the government allowed the Church to organize two nights of preaching at Ben Van Don Gymnasium, District 4, TP. HCM. There were many license and organization procedures. Even before the event, there was a heavy rain, but it didn't stop Christians and their friends who came to the event. Every seat was full, so there were not enough places to stand. The grace of God was not just because some people accepted God but also because the event encouraged and urged many Christian to serve as missionaries.

Ministry Magazine 2011

After that, every year, the Representatives Committee of Ho Chi Minh City continued its evangelism program during Christmas and Easter in Phu Tho and Tao Dan Stadium. There were about 10,000 attendees—thousands of Christians. Thank God, because in the difficult circumstances, God still opened the way for evangelism to be published widely and resonantly, just as the Bible said: "When God opens a door, no one can close it." (Revelation 3:7)

XII. The 45th General Conference of the Federation Church

From 2005–2009, despite facing many difficulties, the Church headed into stability and development. Many groups and churches were re-established, evangelistic work obtained good results, and there was a propensity for education and social health.

Regarding the increasing of the Christians, the representation in the General Council has over 1,000 people, not including informal audiences. Therefore, no one church could have enough room to hold a General Conference. Accordingly, the Board Management of the General Federation had to discuss the work to find a place outside the church to organize. This was the first time in the history of the Evangelical Church in Vietnam that the Church had to find a big enough space for 1,056 formal delegates and thousands of informal attendees. Regarding finances, the space had to be reasonable and government-approved, because this was also a new issue for the government.

Finally, the General Conference of Federation Evangelical Churches of Vietnam (South) took place solemnly March 3–6, 2009 on 116 Nguyen Du Street, Ben Thanh Ward, District 1, Ho Chi Minh City (a sports club). The speaker was Pastor Thai Phuoc Truong, the head pastor of the Church in the South, and Pastor Phung Quang Huyen, the head pastor of the Church in the North.

The General Council voted to re-establish the County mechanism in the organization of the Evangelical Church of Vietnam (South). The classification of churches was also voted in:

- Independent church
- Self-sustaining church
- Branch church (belong to a particular church)

- Groups (belong to the churches)
  Regarding the dignitaries of Vietnamese Evangelical Churches, the titles consisted of:
- Pastor
- New Pastor
- Preacher and Female Preacher
  The Board Management of the Evangelical Church of Vietnam (South) term 2009-2013, as follows:

The Head leader Pastor Thai Phuoc Truong (Re-elected)

Vice Leader I	Pastor Phan Vinh Cu
Vice Leader II	Pastor Ngo Van Buu
General Secretary	Pastor Le Cao Quy
Deputy General Secretary	Pastor Phan Quang Thieu
General Treasurer	Pastor Nguyen Huu Bind
Deputy General Treasurer	Pastor Nguyen Ngoc Thuan

Commissioners

Pastor Siu Y Kim	Pastor Nguyen Van Ngoc
Pastor Chau Van Sang	Preacher Tran Thi Lieu
Pastor Dieu Huynh	Pastor Y Ky Ê Ban
Pastor Phan An Phuoc	Pastor Tran The Thien
Pastor Tran Cong Chanh	Pastor Truong Van Nganh
Pastor Phan Van Cu	Pastor Rmah Loan
Pastor Luu Tu An	Pastor Bui Phung

Pastor Pham Xuan Thieu
(2001-6/2002)

Pastor Duong Thanh
(Interim President 2002-2005)

Pastor Thai Phuoc Truong
(2005-Present)

The head leaders from 2001 to 2011

Pastor Pham Xuan Thieu (2001–2002), Pastor Duong Thanh (as the head leader from June 2002-2005), and Pastor Thai Phuoc Truong (2005 until now)

God's Work in the North of Vietnam

Since 1975, although the country was united, in terms of organization, two regions of the Church had not been united yet. Although there was a desire to communicate, in fact, there were still two separate organizations, which was not contact as it should be. Not until the Evangelical Church of Vietnam (South) had legal status (2001) did the two regions have the chance to visit, meet, and exchange ideas about the unity of the two regions in the future.

Although the Vietnamese Evangelical Church (North) had a status legal from 1963, it was from 1984 that it had the 31st General Conference. It took twenty years to hold the 32nd Conference, when the members of the Board Management of the General Federation had passed away. Hence, activity remained limited and could not develop. The Board Management was very limited when dealing with jobs, both regarding organization and spirituality. The number of pastors and preachers was greatly missed. After more than 20 years, from the previous Bible course (1961–1963), in 1989, the Northern General Federation could open another

Bible course for 15 candidates. Most of these candidates were currently serving God in the churches in the North. Pastor Pham Xuan Thieu and Pastor Nguyen Hau Nhuong from the Vietnamese Evangelical Church (MN) came to participate in teaching.

Tribal Christians

During the wartime from 1954–1975, the Northern Church had suffered so many miseries and challenges, that they are hard to list. Sometimes, it was thought that the Church would gradually be lost, but by the mercy of God and faithfulness of God's children, the Church has remained. However, to date, the Evangelical Church (MB) still has only 14 Kinh churches in 30 churches in the North. Thank God, in recent years, the people of the ethnic group were the most developed, which was the H'Mong and Dao ethnic groups, and the number of Protestant Christians was over 100,000 people. Therefore, in addition to the 14 Official Churches of the Kinh people, there are hundreds of group points for ethnic people in the North. In recent years, some churches have also allowed the government to build new churches to meet the need for God's people to worship.

Before 1954, only a small group of Dao people believed in God because of missionaries in Lang Son province, but the result was not good. Since 1987, many H'mong people have believed in God through radio ministry. At first, their faith was very simple, and they had to go through many difficulties to get in touch with the General Northern Federation to encourage faith and church activities to the present day.

From November 30 to December 2, 2004, the 32nd Conference of General Council was held at Hanoi Church with 150 formal delegates from 15 churches. The new members of the Board Management were:

Head leader	Pastor Phung Quang Huyen
Vice leader	New Pastor Nguyen Gia Huan
Secretary general	New Pastor Au Quang Vinh
General treasurer	New Pastor Nguyen Duc Dong

Commissioners

Pastor Vu Quang Huyen	New Pastor Bui Van San
New Pastor Nguyen Huu Mac	New Pastor Ly Tien Luu
Mr. Trieu Long Tho	Mr. Vu Van Chinh
Mr. Bui Hoanh Thi	Mr. Vu Hong Thai
Female Preacher	Ms. Le Thi Huong Lien

Since 1993, the Northern Church has not opened any theological training course, but the government has allowed the Board of the North General Federation to send students to the Biblical Theology Seminary of the Vietnamese Evangelical Church (South) to educate. From 2007 to present, in three Courses, all 47 students have been trained (Course III: 15 students, Course IV: 14 students, Course V: 18 students, including two female students). These were the official students accepted by both the Church and government. Student graduates will surely become pastors, meeting the need for the dignitaries of the

Northern Church, which was currently lacking personnel.

In addition to the need for the training of God's servants, the need for personnel to take care of group points of ethnic Christians was seriously important. The Board Management was also allowed by the government to open many training classes created for the staff in charge of groups in that time. In the future, these staff members will be supplemented with theology training to meet the need of 100,000 Christians of the Dao ethnic people in the North.

Students from Northern Region – Class 3,4

Closing Ceremony for Biblical Doctrine Class I – 2008-2010

Pastoral Ordination Ceremony – North Region

In general, the Northern Evangelical Church now has the better part of some activities than before. However, the consequences of the past still affected the Church, which had to look at the current situation to obtain the correct direction for the future. The government mostly viewed the following as different organizations: The Southern Vietnamese Evangelical Church (South), The Northern Vietnamese Evangelical Church, and the Highlands Evangelical Church-North-West. In fact, all of these have been one for the last 100 years, from the establishing of the Evangelical Church in Vietnam, because they had the same doctrine and faith. Despite such history, the church has different names, like "Eastern French Evangelical Church," "Eastern France Evangelical Church of Vietnam," "Vietnamese Evangelical Church," and "The Evangelical Church of Vietnam," but the ways, principles, beliefs, and doctrine have remained unchanged. Wishing for that basis, the Vietnamese Church will unite the organization system and its many aspects as well.

The Permanent Members of the General Federation

Head leader	Pastor Nguyen Huu Mac
Vice leader	Pastor Phung Quang Huyen
Secretary	Pastor Bui Van San
Treasurer	Pastor Nguyen Duc Dong
Commissioner	Pastor Hoang Van Luan

Foreign Evangelical Churches

Since the 1975 incident, many Vietnamese people went abroad to other countries in a few ways: migrant, cross-border, union family gathering—they were all Protestant Christians. Although they lived in many different countries, because of the love of God they joined together with God's servants to worship God, preach the Gospel, and develop the Church. Now, many places have established the General Federation, County religion, with the Theological School to train God's servants. Today, the Vietnamese Evangelical Church has been established in many places in America, Europe, Australia, and Asia, or believers keep the traditions of the CM&A while they attend other denominations or independent organizations. Nonetheless, most of the Vietnamese Christians still look to their home church and pray for the development of the Church.

Since 1975, it has not been only the church in the North that has seen development, but also Vietnamese churches in another country. All the Protestant denominations in Vietnam have more than 350 churches, Canada has about 40 churches, Europe has about 42 churches, Australia has 47 churches, and Asia has about 10 churches. In general, in other countries, there have been about 500 churches with the number of Christians about 30,000 people, with 600 pastors and preachers. This was a good thing for “And we know that in all things God works for the good of those who love him.” We hope that millions of Vietnamese people all around the world will hear of God's saving Gospel through the Vietnamese Evangelical Church at home and abroad.

Orange Church – California

Atlanta Church

Church in Singapore

The Private Church and Other Denominations

As mentioned before, the house churches (or private church) are not of the Vietnamese Evangelical Church, but the development of the forms of private church groups have contributed significantly to the mission of the Gospel to many people in recent years, especially through the evangelistic events of Christmas, the Commemoration of the Passion of Christ, and Easter.

In Vietnam, today, there are about 53 active private denominations. Most house churches just sign up members to validate activities that are not yet legal. According to recent statistics, among Protestant Christians (including Vietnamese Evangelical church members and the private church) in the South about 1,300,000 people, or 29 percent, belong to the private denominations, and 71 percent are Christians of the Evangelical Church of Vietnam (also understand as the CM&A).

XIII: Reunification Issue of Two Churches (Southern and Northern)

One of the greatest problems and desires of servants and children of God in the Vietnamese Evangelical Church is the unification of the two religions from the North and South, which have been separated more than half of the last century (57 years) after the Geneva Agreement in 1954. In 1975, the country reunited, but the Vietnamese Evangelical Church (North) and Vietnamese Evangelical Church (South) were still two separate organizations. The 44th Conference of the General Council (2005) of the Vietnamese Evangelical Church (MN) decided to conduct the unification of the Church. The Permanent staff of the General Federation (South) has contacted and sent a charter about this issue to the Board Management of the General Federation (MB), but does not yet expect progress, because there were some obstacles that slowed this process.

After that, the 33rd General Conference of the North (2009) made a resolution on the unification of the two churches. From there, the Permanent staff of Southern churches and The Permanent of Northern churches met several times to discuss and establish the Committee to draft the Charter for the unification of the Church. Finally, The Board of Management of the South and the North agreed together one by one the issues in the Charter. On September 24, 2010, the head leader of the Southern Church (Pastor Thai Phuoc Truong) and the head leader of the Northern Church (Pastor Nguyen Huu Mac) signed the same official document submitted to the Prime Minister and the government's Committee for Religious Affairs for the unification of two churches in the South and North, which has the same name "The Vietnamese Evangelical Church" as before 1954, and also has "The Draft Charter of the Unification," which was approved by The Board Management of the Southern and Northern Church. Now the churches are simply waiting for a reply from the government.

HỘI THÁNH TIN LÀNH VIỆT NAM
(MIỀN BẮC & MIỀN NAM)

Trích yếu: v/v Thống nhất Giáo hội hai miền.

CỘNG HÒA XÃ HỘI CHỦ NGHĨA VIỆT NAM
Độc lập – Tự do – Hạnh phúc

Tp. Hồ Chí Minh, ngày 24 tháng 9 năm 2010

Kính gửi:
- **THỦ TƯỚNG CHÍNH PHỦ**
- **BAN TÔN GIÁO CHÍNH PHỦ.**

Thưa Quí vị,

Thay cho các Tín hữu Tin lành Việt Nam, hai Ban Trị sự Tổng hội *(miền Bắc)* và Tổng liên hội *(miền Nam)*, trân trọng kính chào Thủ tướng và Ban Tôn giáo Chính phủ.

Hội thánh Tin lành Việt Nam đã được thành lập 99 năm qua (1911-2010), đã tồn tại và phát triển với một tín lý, một điều lệ. Vì tình hình đất nước, Giáo hội phải sinh hoạt thành hai tổ chức từ năm 1954. Nước nhà đã thống nhất từ năm 1975, nhưng Giáo hội hai miền vẫn chưa thống nhất.

Nay, căn cứ nhu cầu của toàn thể Tín hữu và thực thi Quyết nghị của Đại Hội đồng Tổng hội lần thứ 33 của Hội thánh miền Bắc và Đại Hội đồng Tổng liên hội lần thứ 44 của Hội thánh miền Nam, chúng tôi kính trình Chính phủ về việc thống nhất Giáo hội với tên chung là Hội thánh Tin lành Việt Nam và Bản dự thảo Hiến chương *(đính kèm)*.

Trân trọng kính trình.

TM. HAI BAN TRỊ SỰ

HỘI TRƯỞNG TỔNG HỘI (miền Bắc)
Mục sư NGUYỄN HỮU MẠC

HỘI TRƯỞNG TỔNG LIÊN HỘI (miền Nam)
Mục sư THÁI PHƯỚC TRƯỜNG

Looking to the Future

First, we give thanks to the One God for His grace and perfect gift to the Vietnamese Evangelical churches after a hundred years. Despite undergoing a century with so many difficulties, the wind and waves hit the boat of the Church, and sometimes, it seemed like the Church could not even exist. Thank God, He has been with the Church through many ups and downs. It is true that God's work was too miraculous for the Evangelical Church of Vietnam in the country as well as overseas. On the occasion of the celebration of a Hundred Years of Gospel in Vietnam, the children and servants of God in the Vietnamese Evangelical Church want to give praise to the Trinity of God and honor His name. The Church also wants to give gratitude to its predecessors for sacrificing their merits, sweat, tears, property, and even their lives to build and develop the Church from its founding until today.

There are countless valuable lessons when reviewing the journey of a hundred years of the work of God in history, especially the Vietnamese Evangelical Church. There is one important point: We cannot forget; the Church must know its past lessons, keep the Church's achievements in the present, and do everything possible for the Church in the future.

Let us praise the Lord for what He has done for His church in the whole past century. On the occasion of the hundredth year since the Gospel came to Vietnam, we must step forward, be content with the orientation the Board Management has issued and inherit the 100-year career of our predecessors. Let us pray, wholeheartedly live in the Gospel, and work to preach, actively build, and develop the Church (According to the report No. 11/2011 BTS / TLH meeting from March 28 to April 1, 2011). We must learn from the history lessons the things God wants to teach us in tears and smiles.

We must always remember the merits of our predecessors that God used to bring Protestantism (the Gospel or the CM&A organization) to Vietnam, to build and develop the church until this very day, hoping God uses these examples to encourage us.

The next generation of the Church today must respect and wholeheartedly keep the good achievements and traditions that our brothers and fathers have left for us. We must make more effort in all areas, do all the work that God assigns to develop the Church for the future, for lost souls who do not know God will be saved to the Church before the Lord's return.

May God give the revision to all God's children and servants as clearly as the prophet in Bible, to serve God as His will, although there will be many huge challenges in the future. The Vietnamese Evangelical Church must thank God for all the amazing grace that God made for His people. However, the development of the Church for a hundred years is still not great compared to the people who have never heard about God in Vietnam and abroad. Therefore, the Church must depend on God and make more efforts to save more people before the Lord's return. The Church must be as equipped as the worthy and pure "bride" who waits for "the groom," who is our Jesus Christ, Our Darling Savior, to come back soon.

I want that wholeheartedly!

--END--

www.ingramcontent.com/pod-product-compliance
Lightning Source LLC
Chambersburg PA
CBHW051344280526
45784CB00007B/2813
* 9 7 8 1 0 9 2 8 5 0 6 7 4 *